MW00949638

I HAVE TODAY

FIND YOUR PASSION, PURPOSE AND SMILE...FINALLY!

DIANE FORSTER

To Robert and Melanie,

Your presence in this world has given my world so much more passion, purpose and never ending smiles! I Love It, Thank It and Bring It every day because of you! My love for you goes beyond what words could ever express. Thank you for being just as you are!

Table of Contents

I HAVE TODAY

I have today to love and be loved.

I have today to be the best I can be.

I have today to pray and meditate.

I have today to learn and grow.

I have today to be open to the possibilities.

I have today to give and share.

I have today to be gentle and kind.

I have today to start fresh and new.

I have today to nurture my spirit, mind and body.

I have today to watch my dreams come true.

I have today to see things with new eyes.

I have today to live abundantly and fearlessly.

I have today to be more beautiful than yesterday.

I have today...Thank You, God, for today.

Diane Forster

8/24/13

WELCOME TO 'I HAVE TODAY'

I want to say welcome! I am so excited that you are here and you are now part of my "family." We are going to take this journey together to find your passion, your purpose, and your smile again.

It is going to be a fun journey. We are going to uncover things and unlock so many wonderful qualities about you that have been hidden for a long, long time. I can't wait for you to get started!

I want you to know that during this process you are going to be going on a roller coaster ride of sorts. There will be highs, there will be lows, and probably some tears shed. There will be moments of uncovering things about me…and yourself that you may not want to acknowledge. But, that's all really good! I promise you, you'll be different. You'll feel happier.

The online course is designed to take ninety days. But with all the lessons available, you can take as much or as little time as you need to get through it. At the end you will wake up feeling lighter and better, like you lost ten pounds…ten pounds of old stuff! Each and every day you are going to feel stronger, more empowered, and more like the person that you were meant to be, and that you know that you are.

So, stay the course but know that you are not alone. I'm here to support you! I would recommend that you make your time to do this work a sacred time, calendar it and make it a priority in your life.

This is an investment in you and your path back to the life that you want to live. Also know that you can ask questions at any time, at any point during the journey by emailing me.

I can't wait to get started with you and I can't wait to see what your passion is, and to see your smile returning again. Share your comments and your progress with us on the site, and let's get started with the "I Have Today" System.

This is called the "I Have Today" System because we live in the present moment. Our lives are lived today, right now, in this moment. The past is behind us, and the future is unknown. We spend too much of our lives living in the past and worrying about the future, when the moment is right now. It is TODAY.

I have today to shine. I have today to love. I have today to be open to new things. I have today to nurture my spirit, mind, and body. I have today to be the best that I can be.

I Have Today was created from a poem that I wrote (in the front of the book). You can download it from our website as well. Print it and use it as your mantra, like I do. I live by this mantra, and I hope that you will too, because it keeps reminding me to stay present and this is our moment, right now. We have today and I am so happy to share this day with you.

With Love!

Diane

For more information, go to www.dianeforster.com or www.ihavetoday.com. Enter your name and email address to become part of the "I Have Today" Community, and receive FREE gifts, like the "I Love You" Chant and the "I Forgive You" Chant.

DIANE'S STORY

Many have asked me about my story and how I got where I am today. I'll share a little bit about my journey and get real about where I was and where I am today. I will start back in the beginning, with a little history about me.

Just briefly, I grew up in New York, until I was 17. We moved around a lot. I am one of three girls, and I am the middle sister. My mom and dad loved each other deeply, but they struggled in their relationship. I didn't witness that romantic kind of loving experience between them. I remember when I was 24, my parents separated for the last time and finally decided they were going to divorce. They loved each other so much, but they just couldn't live together.

I was 24 years old when my father told me that he loved me for the first time. That had a powerful impact on me. I remember the moment vividly. I was standing in my apartment bedroom in my place in Venice, California and I was talking to him on the phone. Talk about having a profound moment! I felt it everywhere! I KNEW he loved me, but I had never heard those words before.

The lesson I received in that experience was understanding his perspective, how big that moment must have been for him, and how little love he probably witnessed in his life. How few times he heard the words 'I love you'? I will say that ever since that day, I hear those words from him every day. It was a transformational moment for him, and a lesson for me. I am learning from that example.

That barely, but briefly describes the sort of relationship they had.

We moved from New York to California the summer before my senior year of high school. It was an extremely traumatic emotional time for me because I had to leave behind what I considered to be an amazing life. I was popular, I had a boyfriend I loved, I was really involved in Student Council and dancing, and I loved my life. I was plucked out of that environment and put into a strange new world to me. We moved to Encino, California, surrounded by so much wealth all around us.

I grew up in a small town on Long Island. We were middle class, but I felt rich. I felt there wasn't anything that I wanted and didn't have. And now I was exposed to a world where there was a lot of money everywhere. It really created some huge money issue hang ups for me, to be honest. That is where I discovered my lack of wealth issues, and lack of value issues.

I've discovered major breakthroughs about that time in my life. I uncovered and pinpointed issues I have about feeling like I wasn't good enough, I wasn't worthy. That is a struggle that I know a lot of you out there have. I am going to show you down the road on our journey together how you can unlock that because I know what that feels like.

That year, the number one lesson for me was to be open for newness. I didn't want to leave behind that life. That life was nice, it was comfortable, it was easy, I had it all figured out. But, then I had to stretch myself and create new friendships, new relationships, and learn a lot about things that initially I was not interested in.

Honestly, I made life for my parents very difficult that year because it was not something that I wanted to do. I wasn't given a choice. That said, I ended up creating great friendships. In fact, two of my best friends to this day were women I met that senior year of high school. I definitely looked for and found the gift in that situation. We are still close friends to this day.

After graduating high school I went off to college. I found out pretty quickly that college was not for me. I went for one year, and I was sick a lot that year. I spent three weeks in and out of the health center. I suffered pneumonia and it was a tough year for me. So, when I came home after freshman year, I had decided that it was not the path that I was going to take.

I took a different path thinking I wanted to be a court reporter because I heard that court reporters made a lot of money. That was the "sizzle" for me. Over that summer, I took a temporary job as a secretary since I had taken a lot of clerical classes in high school. I was good at that. I was skilled to do that. I applied at a temporary agency and got a job at an advertising agency in LA.

It was supposed to be a two-week temp job. Well, that job became a career for me. They offered me a full-time position. I remember at that time, it was for $13,000 dollars a year. It felt like it was a million dollars. It could have well been back in that day. I decided to take that job and not return to college. I took classes at night to become a court reporter, because that was still my desire.

After two years of working in advertising full-time and going to school full-time at night, I realized that court reporting was not for me. I did NOT have the personality to just sit behind a machine all day, being quiet, taking down the dictation of what other people were saying.

So, I explored my options in the agency. I thought since I had a foot in the door here, how I could maximize this opportunity? I was not going to go back to college. What could I do for myself? I pursued a position in media and that sent me down the path to work in media in many different roles. I did that for about eight years. Along the path, I discovered that I was sitting on the wrong side of the desk.

Just like court reporting wasn't right, the media buyer side of the desk wasn't right anymore either; I wanted to be on the sales side. They were making a lot more money, working way less hours, and were having a lot more fun! I decided, in that moment, that I wanted to pursue a sales position at some point in the near future.

There were two companies I wanted to work for. They were Group W and ABC. I considered them the best, so that was my goal.

Time was moving along, and then I met my husband who lived in Chicago. We dated long distance, back and forth, from LA to Chicago, for two and half years. Back and forth, back and forth, until we decided that I would be the one to move to Chicago. I left my job, and my family, and the career path I was on for a man. I left for love. I know some of you have done that too.

It was a blessing in disguise, because three months after I left and quit that amazing job, the agency lost several of their major accounts. Six months later the entire media department was let go. My timing was perfect.

Another lesson...take those leaps of faith!!! I decided this is what I wanted. I want this man, I want a marriage, and I want children. So, I put that priority first and I went for it.

When I moved to Chicago, it was then I made the commitment to get into sales. I hustled. I hit the streets hard. I went to every TV station in town, every radio station in town, every rep firm in town. I hit it really hard. It took me about three months to land a job at a company called Telerep. It was a grind, and it was tough. But working there gave me amazing sales skills. I learned so much while I was there.

I worked there for over two years, honing my skills, building relationships and learning the business. Then, one day, I got a phone call from the manager at Group W (one of the places I said I wanted to work for) telling me she had heard amazing things about me in town, she had an opening, she was leaving, and a new manager was coming in. She wanted me to come in to meet him and pitch the job. I went in, interviewed for the position and got the job on the spot! If any of you are familiar with this industry, then you know that kind of thing just does not happen. People don't leave those jobs. The competition is fierce. Yet, I walked in and get the job on the spot…with a huge pay raise! I was doing a happy dance! I remember thinking that I had set that intention many years before, and now it was coming to fruition.

I worked at Group W for a few years. Then Westinghouse bought CBS, and Group W and CBS TV Sales merged. I really didn't like the dynamics that were going on in the company since the merger. We merged offices together and things were changing. I was only there for about six weeks when, guess what? I got a phone call from a friend at ABC. She called to say "We have an opening, I told my manager all about you, and I think you should come and talk with him about the job". I immediately went into action and called the manager right away. I went through a very short interview process and got the job offer a little over a week after my interview.

The two places I said I wanted to work for I ultimately did. That is the power of manifestation! That is the power of our word! You need to watch your words because what you say will come into your life; you will manifest it right in! I was manifesting when I didn't even know what manifestation was…but I was doing it! I was so blessed in the career area of my life.

Now, let me talk about my marriage. My ex and I married back in the early 1990s. Things were good initially. You know, when you are at that time in your life…excited about everything…about the wedding, and the planning, and the day. It wasn't at all about "the marriage." I'm guessing many of you can relate to that.

I spent so much time focused on the day but not about what the actual marriage was going to look like. I spent a lot of time in that marriage thinking that things were going to get better. Once we get through the wedding, then things will get better, and when we find where we are going to live then things will get better, and when we have kids then things will get better.

Well, things were not getting better. They were cycling up and down. There were a lot of moments of the marriage that were good, but there were many, many dark moments. I just kept telling myself, "things will be better." but they were not getting better.

When my ex-husband and I decided we were going to start trying for a baby, we had difficulty. I think part of the difficulty was he really didn't want kids; he was only doing it for me. After six months of trying, we went in for testing. We found out that he was fine, and I was the one with the problem.

I started a process of surgeries, drugs, testing, ultrasounds, frequent doctor appointments, you name it. At the same time I was going through fertility issues, my mom was sick and dying from colon cancer. I went through one of the darkest times of my life. I was flying back and forth to LA helping my sister and my dad with my mom, taking her to appointments and helping her with her chemo treatments. Meanwhile, I was squeezing in all of those procedures, drugs, ultrasounds, and surgeries for my infertility back in Chicago. This was also at the same time that I switched my career from working at CBS to ABC. I had the perfect storm going on all at once, and I just didn't know which way was up. I was in a sort of zombie mode. I was just functioning and getting through each day. I wanted these things so badly in my life, and I was forging forward through it.

I decided something had to give. I wanted to have children. I wanted my mother to see me as a mother. It was something that was really important to me. But, I guess God had other plans. I had to give up that need of control. That need to make that happen on MY time. My mom passed away on October 1st, 1996 and I became pregnant the very next month.

I believe part of the reason it happened that way was my mom needed her wings. She was (and is) now my angel. I know her…she put her first order of business in heaven to tell God to give her daughter a baby…in fact, give her two! It really was a blessing in disguise. I see that the gift of me being pregnant right after my mother passed away truly was a gift because I was grieving her passing so badly. This was giving me something to have hope for. I gave birth to my twins nine months later and that path itself was quite a journey.

Not only did I struggle conceiving my twins, I also struggled during the pregnancy. I was put on bed rest at 30 weeks. The doctors told me 'you just need to get to 32 weeks'. So, 32 weeks came and went, and then 33 weeks came and went, 34 weeks, 35, 36, 37, 38, 39 weeks! After all that, I went full term and even needed to be induced! I'm not kidding!

I couldn't believe that after all that, my wonderful reward was that God blessed me with two healthy babies – a boy and a girl…so perfect and beautiful!

During the baby years and toddler years, that time was all a blur. If any of you mothers out there can relate, then you know what I'm talking about…it is all about them. That is just what life is all about. I did my best to get committed, get organized, and raise these twins in a way that allowed me to have some normalcy in my life. I put some systems in place to keep them on a schedule and to keep me on a schedule. I'm so anal and obsessive compulsive, and those "skills" served me back in those years. I had GREAT babies…I was blessed.

With my ex and me, our relationship was struggling as it was, but it really went on the back burner at that time. Life becomes about our kids. I know this happens a lot. I talk to a lot of people who say that their whole life revolves around their kids. Their kids are in their bed at night, and their relationships suffer greatly because of that. It is a struggle to keep any sense of passion or intimacy in the relationship.

As the years went on, more and more of our life just became friendly. Our marriage, our relationship was just friendship, and it was all about our children. Everything we did, to the outside world, looked rosy and happy. We looked like we had the perfect life; the husband, the wife, the son, the daughter, two dogs, everything looking happy and beautiful. Yet, on the inside it was imploding, and I was dying more and more and more every day.

I completely lost my sense of femininity, sexiness, passion, and drive. I looked at myself in the mirror and looked old. I was carrying extra weight, I was losing my shape. I lost my passion for sex. I just honestly didn't care about my love life. My passion was put on the back burner, and I was putting me on the back burner. It got to the point where I just couldn't take it anymore.

My soul and spirit were slipping away moment by moment by moment, day by day.

I attempted to take my life. I found myself in the bathroom late one night. It started out as a typical day, you know, business as usual, taking care of the kids, going over to some friends' house for a barbeque. There were several families there, and everything looked perfect on the outside. But, as soon as we left, the fighting ensued, and I just didn't feel any love or support from my spouse at all anymore. There was nothing.

I went up to the bathroom, and I locked the door. I grabbed two bottles of pills, and I was going to end my life because I just couldn't take the pain anymore. I couldn't bare the loneliness and emptiness another moment. I couldn't take another day like that. We had been drinking quite a bit of sangria and wine that night, which made the situation worse. There were two full bottles of pills emptied out into my hand. I looked down at them, then something much greater than me karate chopped my arm and knocked those pills out of my hand and all over the floor. A voice so clearly whispered into my ear, "Oh

12

no, Diane, you are not ending it this way! This is not the end of your story. You have so much more to do! You need to help yourself, and you need to help others." I took a breath, I wiped my tears, I looked up and I said, "Okay. Show me the way!"

I cleaned up the mess, took all of the pills and flushed them down the toilet, composed myself, left the bathroom, hugged and kissed my children good night and went to bed. The next day, I woke up and said, "I am changing my life! I have got to get help!"

I called a therapist and said I need help. I had to do something! I couldn't do this alone! My counselor and I worked deeply on some of the issues. We were building up my strength, helping me to prepare myself for how I was going to live life. How was I going to live a life on my own? Could I do that, because it had been years and years since I'd done that? How was I going to support myself financially? How were the kids going to adapt? What was all this going to look like?

All of these were unknown elements and honestly, filled with so much fear. I was so afraid of what the outside world was going to think. What were my family and friends all going to think? Who is going to judge me? Everybody? We look like we have this perfect family. I have tried, and tried, and tried to make things work with this man. I know, there were parts of him that were trying too. But I couldn't do it anymore.

Here is where it gets real. I kept stalling. I kept delaying. Why was I pausing? What was I so afraid of? Why couldn't I just take that leap? I had taken leaps in the past. I knew the net would always be there. I knew how to take a leap, but why I couldn't take this leap? The whispers kept getting louder and louder and louder, until one day I discovered my ex was having an affair.

It was the Saturday after Thanksgiving. My daughter and I were at home decorating the house for Christmas. I was in search of an extension cord, but I couldn't find one. I looked downstairs, the basement, the garage. I finally went into my husband's office to see whether he had one. It was there that I discovered what every woman doesn't want to discover. There were signs everywhere of the affair. There was a perfume bottle that clearly was not mine, there were pictures, there were emails, and there were cards and notes. I mean, it was all exposed right there.

It was as if it was calling me like a beacon, shouting, "Come look over here!' In many ways, I feel like he wanted to be caught. My heart sank; I couldn't breathe. My daughter was downstairs waiting for me to do this beautiful tradition we had done for years. This wonderful holiday tradition, one of many that we created throughout their lives, and I couldn't get out of the chair.

I could not move. I could not breathe. But I had to. I had to pull it together. So I did, I pulled it together, went downstairs, and continued to decorate the tree. Shortly thereafter, I took my daughter over to a friend's house. Now, I was in the car by myself, and I lost it! I called my therapist to reach for help but I couldn't get her on the phone since it was a holiday weekend. I called my sisters to reach out for help, but they were with family since it was a holiday weekend. I had this huge revelation, this huge uncovering, this huge A-Ha, here it is…slapped in my face right in front of me, and I had no one to turn to.

I turned to myself and said "well, here it is Diane." The gift in all of this was that, in that moment, I was enraged! I was pissed! This was the final straw I needed to cut the cord and release myself from any attachment to this man. We were done! And I was going to see an attorney on Monday to do something about it. I had this gift from God that released me. Yes, it IS a gift!

I needed to get to that place of anger so that I could cut it. If any one of you has been there then you know that feeling. You need that push over the edge, and that was the push that I needed. That was an empowering moment for me. Don't get me wrong…it was ugly, it was hard, it was brutal. There was denial from him. I had all the proof in the world that it had been going on for years! It was all right there. Yet, I still got denial from him. Even then, in that moment, my thoughts were "I am still receiving nothing from him in terms of trust."

So…in that moment, I took care of me. It was an empowering moment that set me down the path to "I can do this, I can do this, I can do this. I can take care of me."

So, what's the first thing you have to do when you realize this? Now I have to tell people. I have to tell the world my story. I have to tell them that this perfect marriage is not so perfect. I am leaving my husband. That is the hardest part…getting the words out and telling people. What surprised me, and I don't know why, was the tremendous amount of support I received.

Here is the reality—the more honest, upfront, vulnerable, and authentic you are with your story, the more people can't talk about you. There is no gossip; you are being yourself and people praise that. People want to help you. They want to be there for you.

That was a very enlightening moment for me. It helped me and supported me so much on my path to living my life without my husband and no longer being a "Mrs." That was a tremendous gift to me, and an aid to me. I was going to live on my own and be living with my children part-time, and they would be living with their dad part-time…and it was all going to be fine!

While on my own then, I decided to do some deep, deep digging into myself. I did a lot of work and I spent so much time learning, reading every book I could on personal development, spiritual growth, and empowerment. I watched everything I could, listened to everything I could, and I decided that this was an opportunity to educate myself and learn where I fell short in that relationship—and other relationships.

What was I doing that contributed to the demise of that relationship? Because, let's face it, yes, there was deception and betrayal, a breach of trust and many of those things. But, I was an enabler, I was enabling this, I was allowing this. Why would I allow myself be treated that way or not treated that way?

Also, what deep issues did I have to uncover about myself and my behaviors so that I wouldn't repeat that pattern? I didn't want to invite that sort of relationship in my life again. I wanted to live a life much richer than that. I wanted a beautiful, romantic, intimate relationship. I wanted fulfilling relationships in all areas of my life; I wanted happiness in all areas of my life as well. I wanted to be fulfilled in my career, in family, in relationships, everywhere!

What were my issues? That is why I have done all of this work. All of this research into "I Have Today." That is how I discovered "I Have Today." I woke up one day with that poem and mantra in my head. I got it all down on a piece of paper and said to myself, "This is something. I Have Today. This is a calling. I am supposed to make people feel good. I am supposed to serve people. And give them their passion, and purpose, and their smile back. I am going to find mine and I have today to do it."

That is when all of this came to me; that is what empowered me. I realized that the past is irrelevant. Let me heal in the best, most effective, permanent way possible so that I can move on with my life and live the life of my dreams. Now, I am in a place where I AM living the life of my dreams. I left behind a life of living in this unhappy, unhealthy relationship where I was unfulfilled and unhappy with certain areas of my life and doing it mostly for my kids.

I was dreading each day. I would literally put my feet on the floor in the morning and be tired and exhausted. Ugh, another day to get through, living for the weekend. When you live like that, you are never living in the present moment. Now, however, fast forward to where I am.

I am passionate every day; my feet hit the floor and I am excited, I throw my arms up in the air and shout, "I love my life, I love my life, I love my life! Yes, yes, yes! What miracles are open to me today? Bring It!" I love the uncertainty of life! I am living this incredibly empowered life. I manifested this amazing life! I DID THIS! I went from living in Chicago in a house that I had lived in for 20 years, where my kids were raised, to selling that house, quitting my corporate job, getting rid of all my belongings, and moving to California to start a new chapter of my life!

I live at the beach; I look at the ocean every single day. I watch the beautiful sunsets. I work for myself. I am building empires! Is there any fear associated with this? Yes! But, I'm doing it anyway! I am creating wealth, financial freedom, and I'm living life the way it's supposed to be lived! It's supposed to be FUN!

I've taken years to be able to live this way through my hard work and study. Now, I invite you to follow me, and follow my example because I am making it easy for you. You will be able to do this easily with my three-step processes that will get you where you want to be! I promise you, your life is going to change in ways that you could never have imagined. But, you MUST believe it can. Let me guide you on this journey, let's do this together, let's become a community together, let's become a tribe together, let's support one another.

I am here for you. I am happy to share this story with you of my journey, because we all have our story. We all have our stuff; that is just part of our path. I mean, we are here and it is not all good, it is not always pretty, but it could be so much better. The dark days, and the negativity, and the stuff that brings us down, doesn't have to be who we are. We can easily turn that around to be impassioned, enlightened women, and people in general...if we see the GIFT in everything.

What we need to do is do it in a way that serves us. By serving us, we serve others. So that we empower others by our example, by showing our grace, our passion, lighting up as we enter a room, by our purpose being what drives us, and by our smile that gives us energy in our life; and that energy spreads like wildfire!

We truly can't serve others until we take care of ourselves. It is like being on the airplane with the oxygen mask; they tell you right away, first put your mask on before helping anybody else. There is great truth to that statement. We must breathe life into ourselves before we can we take care of others.

We have to be healthy physically, emotionally, mentally, financially, and in our relationships. We serve others when we ourselves are taken care of. Let me give you an example.

I really didn't start serving others until I really took care of myself. Yes, did I do what I needed to do to take care of my kids? Yes. Did I do my family obligations? Yes. Did I perform my job to the level that I could do at that time? Yes. I did what I needed to do, but there wasn't much passion in most of that.

Until I really started taking care of myself and listening to me and doing for me...nurturing my mind, my body, my spirit and focusing on what my needs were and how to take care of me fully and completely...was I able to really start serving others. It wasn't initially in any grand way; it was just in what I was doing and how I was showing up.

I started looking better and speaking better and offering advice in a very effortless way, because I had done all of this work. I read so many books, I learned all of these techniques, and I saw that my path to helping myself was having this ripple effect on those around me. I was actually finding I had more time in my life, not less time. I was doing more for me. I was literally being selfish in a really good way, and I had actually created more time in my life. I had time to do more of the things that I wanted to do.

I took care of my obligations but I took care of me easily and effortlessly. I know that time management is such a big thing for us. We feel like there is not enough time. Wouldn't it be great if *you* managed time instead of time managing you? That was one of the things I have learned on this path. So, I want to close this chapter by offering you this.

Exercise:

Here is one thing you can do today to set you on your path of self-discovery and nurturing to live the kind of life that you really want to live…full of passion, purpose, and creating your constant smile. I want you to carve out some time. How much? Twenty minutes, an hour maybe. Grab yourself a cup of coffee or tea, go sit somewhere quietly, and write out your ideal life. What your life looks like in your mind…the way you WANT it to look.

What you look like in that life. What your family looks like. What your career looks like. What all of your relationships look like. What your surroundings look like. Your home, your car, your kids, your pets, your spare time, your vacations, traveling. What are you doing for fun? Are you exercising or playing sports? Put down every intricate detail. Make it as beautiful and as expansive as you want to be. Go big, dream the beautiful life that you desire and you deserve. Remember, you are limited by NOTHING in this infinite universe!

Then, I want you to sit in that moment with it and FEEL how good that feels! Stay in that state for as long as possible. While you're in that state, the universe is "going to work" on your desires.

When you're finished with it, put it in a place where you can read it every night before you go to bed for three weeks. It takes 21 days to form a new habit. Start there. We are going to get the momentum going and flowing, and we are beginning with this one small task.

You'll start to notice that as you are entering your dream state while falling sleep, (into that place where you are at a highly elevated level envisioning your life as you WANT it to be and not how it is) that this will start to expand you. You are going to wake up feeling better, more energized, more inspired, and happier. I promise you, do that for three weeks and watch how much better you're going to begin to feel. You'll really start to see some shifts! Have FUN!

Chapter Summary
In this chapter we learned:
• Diane's childhood, young ages, relations with parents.
• The gifts in every experience.
• Challenges with marriage, facing distrust, and empowerment.

For more information, go to www.dianeforster.com or www.ihavetoday.com. Enter your name and email address to become part of the "I Have Today" Community, and receive FREE gifts, like the "I Love You" Chant and the "I Forgive You" Chant.

DIANE'S MEDITATIONS

RAINBOW MEDITATIONS ™

I have been meditating for a long time…several years. I have tried many different practices. I listen to guided meditations, meditation soundtracks, nature sounds, pure silence, for example. I developed the Rainbow series of meditations, because it was something that seemed to work better for me overall.

I could fit into my daily practice. It is something I can do anywhere at any time, and I receive many benefits from it. It sort of just spoke to me one day, and it has evolved over time.

I perfected it and added on the different layers to it to the point now where I feel like it is a really good, rich meditation practice that serves me extremely well. I hope that it serves you, and I hope that you get great benefit from it.

If it's not something that works for you, I would strongly advise you try to find one that does fit and work for you. The reason is, without question, meditation has been the paramount ritual that has had the most powerful impact on my life. By adding meditation to my life, it has really changed who I am. I approach life in such a calm manner, because my vibration is so elevated.

People constantly say to me "you are so chill, nothing ever rattles you. How is that possible?" Trust me, I used to not be like that! I would be the first to fly off the handle and have such a short trigger. Now…nothing rattles me.

For the most part, I handle everything with calmness and ease. Now, I definitely *respond* versus *react*, which is huge! I contribute that one hundred percent to meditation. I can't encourage you enough to take on a form of meditation--whether it is my practice or one that you discover on your own.

There are two types of Rainbow Meditations: Rainbow Breaths and Rainbow Ribbon of Healing. I hope that you find mine useful but if not, please, look into the many other options. There are free meditations all over the Internet. You can try anything and check it out to see if it works for you. That is how these came about for me, and how and why I developed them. My hope is that they work for you.

Chapter Summary

In this chapter we learned:
• Diane's meditations.
• Positive effects of mediation.
• How meditation leads to calmness.

RAINBOW BREATH MEDITATION ™

Before you begin any meditation practice, get in a comfortable position, hands on your lap, facing down or facing up—either way will work. You can sit on the floor if you want. I don't recommend you lay down because people tend to fall asleep when they lay down. It's most important to be comfortable.

The Rainbow Breath meditation is very effective in making me feel amazing! Think of the process as 4-8-8-4. Take in a breath for four seconds, imagining a rainbow mist of color filling you up. You then send that mist to each chakra, one at a time, beginning with your root chakra. (There are wonderful chakra center grids all over the Internet that show you which chakra is connected to which primary function, principles, body parts, emotions, etc. They go into much greater detail than I am doing here. However, just know that when you do my Rainbow Meditation Process, you're energizing ALL of them...creating perfect balanced health!)

You breathe in for the count of four, and you are breathing in that rainbow mist with all that beautiful color. You will already start to feel really good in your body because of the oxygenation. Just breathe in. Now, hold that breath for the count of eight as you then imagine lighting up all of your chakras one at the time...each one using the colors of the rainbow that you just inhaled.

> Your root chakra is your base chakra, which is red.
>
> Your sacral chakra is right in the middle area between your belly button and your root chakra, and that one is orange.
>
> Your solar plexus is right in the middle of your stomach by your navel, which is yellow.
>
> Your heart chakra (you know where your heart is!), is green.

Your throat chakra lies at the base of your throat, and the color is blue.

Your third eye chakra lies right in between your eyes, and that color is indigo.

Your crown chakra is at the top of your head, and that color is violet.

Then, we add your soul star chakra, which is anywhere from 6 inches to two feet above your crown chakra. The color is white.

Once you're breathed in the rainbow mist for four seconds, hold it as you light up each chakra, one by one to the count of eight, and just imagine the bright colors of the rainbow. Lighting them up. Igniting them. Red-root, orange-sacral, yellow-solar plexus, green-heart, blue-throat, indigo-third eye, violet-crown, white-soul star.

The last step is to breathe out for eight seconds like you are blowing out birthday candles on a birthday cake. (Your abdomen will feel a bit like a deflated balloon when you are finished…and that's really healthy! Holding your breath like that oxygenates your blood.) Now, while you are breathing out, I want you to imagine what you're blowing out is any old toxic soot, waste, negative memories and energy, old wounds, fear…anything that no longer serves you. Imagine what is coming out is smoky and ugly. It's gone. It's released from you forever!

I do this process a minimum of four times. (The easiest way I remember the whole process is 4-8-8-4. 4 breaths in, 8 seconds to hold and light up my chakras, 8 seconds to breathe out and release, do it 4 times.) I always feel so calm and peaceful afterwards. It's incredibly healing!

Chapter Summary

In this chapter we learned:

• What is rainbow breath meditation?
• The importance of lighting up your chakras and 4-8-8-4.

For more information, go to www.dianeforster.com or www.ihavetoday.com. Enter your name and email address to become part of the "I Have Today" Community, and receive FREE gifts, like the "I Love You" Chant and the "I Forgive You" Chant.

Rainbow Ribbon of Healing ™

After I complete the Rainbow Breaths, I do what I call the Rainbow Ribbon of Healing. With the Rainbow Ribbon of Healing, think of a figure eight. A figure eight looks like the number eight, right? It's also the Infinity sign. You want to imagine a rainbow ribbon wrapping around the torso of your body in a figure eight. Do it in two directions. Do it from front to back, then from side to side.

This is a simple process. Sit in the same position as the Rainbow Breaths Meditation. Close your eyes. Now, imagine there's a beautiful, thick, transparent, rainbow ribbon (similar to stained glass...it's solid, but you can see through it) that begins at the front of your throat chakra, then rounds through your body at your solar plexus (naval area) through the other side around your lower back until it reaches your root chakra. Then, it comes back up your front through your solar plexus and back out your upper back area until it connects back up to your throat chakra. That's a figure 8. Infinity sign.

Do each of the four moves to the count of 4. (1-upper front; 2-lower back; 3-lower front; 4-upper back.) Make sense? (There's a video demonstration in the "I Have Today System" online course.)

Next Step: Do that same scenario left to right instead of front to back. Do it to the count of 4. (1-upper left; 2-lower right; 3-lower left; 4-upper right.)

Just keep going front to back, then side to side, counting 1-2-3-4, 1-2-3-4. Continue doing this for 10-15 minutes.

That is all there is to it. You can do this with music if it helps you do it. There is really no wrong way to do it. Just visualize there is a big giant rainbow ribbon, and you are wrapping yourself in love. Healing energy and love. It is so POWERFUL! Beautiful colors of the rainbow. The synchronicity is in the fact that you are thinking about a rainbow ribbon as your visualization, and the color of your chakras are the same colors of the rainbow. That's alignment. Your chakras are already lit up from the rainbow breaths feeling healing energy. Now they are being wrapped in a ribbon of healing love.

Think about it…if you are sending healing energy to every one of your chakras every day, you can't help but feel good! You are going continue to feel better, and better, and better! Each and every time you do this, you will feel the positive effects.

As you are doing the meditation, keep your mind on the colors and on the counting. The counting is a very effective tool for meditation because it keeps your mind focused on the meditation, keeping your presence where you are (versus allowing all things you have to do, all things you have to take care of, all that outside chatter from coming in.)

You just stay with the counting – 4,8,8,4 with the rainbow breaths, and just keep counting to four with the rainbow ribbon.

You want to apply these meditation practices into your life in terms of health, money, your love life, relationships, family, career and whatever else may be. Set an intention at the start of your meditation practice of whatever area of your life you want to focus on that day. Say it is love; and you want to focus on intimate love, romantic love, divine love. Say aloud, "I set the intention with this meditation to heal any negative energy I have connected with romantic love. Any old contracts I have with them, I erase, clear and delete them. I set the intention to have divine, romantic, intimate love. Thank you."

By setting that intention, it is focused on positive energy, clearing out and getting rid of any of those old negative energies that you might be carrying around, related to whatever your topic or your issue is.

Lastly, have fun with it! Enjoy this sacred ritual!

Chapter Summary
In this chapter we learned:
• What is rainbow ribbon of healing?
• The synchronicity of rainbow and chakra colors.
• The importance of counting to keep you focused.

For more information, go to www.dianeforster.com or www.ihavetoday.com. Enter your name and email address to become part of the "I Have Today" Community, and receive FREE gifts, like the "I Love You" Chant and the "I Forgive You" Chant.

SETTING INTENTIONS

We touched on this at the end of the last chapter. Setting intentions is also a very important part of this meditation practice, and setting intentions is easy. All you do is verbally speak and acknowledge what it is you would like to get out of the experience, or your day, or your life. An intention is how you want to live; this is the easiest way to say it.

Here are some examples. I set the intention today that I am going to hit every green light when I am driving, and I get a parking spot in front wherever I go. I set the intention that I am going to eat really healthy today. I set the intention that I am going to smile at every stranger I see. Those are all intentions.

They could be as simple or as grand as you want them to be. By setting an intention into your practice it anchors it and grounds it. It gives you the opportunity to really carry it with you and makes it a lot easier for it to actually come to fruition.

I have heard a lot in past that people say, "I don't know to meditate, it doesn't work for me. I can't sit there"...whatever it is. I can understand if you are new to meditation, it may seem weird and foreign to you, and a little uncomfortable. But, it just takes a little practice. Ease into it and know this for a certainty...you can't do it wrong! There is no way to do it wrong.

Put yourself at ease and relax. You are not going to screw it up. It's all going be okay. I am going give you a couple of quick, simple intentions that you can bring into your life right now. We can build on them later, or you can build on them anyway you see fit. Just incorporate whatever works for your life.

Example: I set the intention today to be open and optimistic. Easy, right? I mean, that is generic and it's not attached to anything. Be easy on yourself. Don't start out with something really big that if it doesn't happen, you're going to feel bad about it. Keep them simple.

Other examples: I set the intention today to tell five people that I love them. I set the intention today to show up to my life a hundred percent. I set the intention today to do something kind for a perfect stranger. I set the intention today to do one thing that makes me uncomfortable…because I know it will stretch me. That might be one thing you want to do down the road. Give it a try, it can't hurt, right?

Remember, you can't get it wrong. You are taking action, and you are reaching for something. So, it is ALL GOOD!

Chapter Summary
In this chapter we learned:
• How to set right intentions.
• Start out with simple, generic intentions.
• You can't get it wrong, so have fun.

For more information, go to www.dianeforster.com or www.ihavetoday.com. Enter your name and email address to become part of the "I Have Today" Community, and receive FREE gifts, like the "I Love You" Chant and the "I Forgive You" Chant.

THREE-STEP PROCESS – LOVE IT! THANK IT! BRING IT!

Let me introduce to you the three-step process. Why is it three steps? Because it is easy! I spent so much time and energy perfecting this system so that it will be easy for you to incorporate into your life.

The three steps are LOVE IT! THANK IT! BRING IT!

The first step is to LOVE IT! By loving it, you acknowledge that there are no wasted moments in this life: the good, the bad, the beautiful, the ugly, all of it, it is a treasured gift because it opens us and expands us. If we don't experience difficult things, then we wouldn't know how to gain clarity for the things we really want out of life.

You must love each moment of your life! I mean...it's your life, for goodness sake, and that in itself is a gift! By loving every moment, that gets you closer and closer to who you are every single day. With that clarity, you get better and better with each new day. I will show you how.

The second step is to THANK IT! This is where gratitude and appreciation come in. We all need to be grateful for everything in our life. I will take you through the process of what 'thank it' is and how to incorporate gratitude into all areas of your life.

The final step is to BRING IT! This is where your empowerment comes in. You have loved your life; you have thanked your life now you've got to "bring it" on for your life. How are you "showing up" in your life? Throughout the book, I'll talk a lot about how you "show up" in your life contributes to your happiness.

Are you giving it your all? Are you jumping out of the bed enthused about the day or are you dreading getting out of bed? Are you bringing enthusiasm into cooking dinner? Are you bringing enthusiasm into doing laundry? Are you bringing joy into your work? Are you bringing happiness into your life with your relationships? This is a very important part of the process. This determines how quickly things shift for you.

I've made this so easy and simple. It will be an effortless flow for you to take action for your life that's going to cause massive results because I'm giving you a road map with step- by-step directions. Are you ready? Let's go!

Chapter Summary
In this chapter we learned:
• What is the three-step process.
• Love every moment of your life.
• How are you showing up in your life?

For more information, go to www.dianeforster.com or www.ihavetoday.com. Enter your name and email address to become part of the "I Have Today" Community, and receive FREE gifts, like the "I Love You" Chant and the "I Forgive You" Chant.

LOVE IT – EXPLAINED

Let me talk about love. How much of your life do you actually love? You know there are no wasted moments. Are you loving the bed that you sleep in? Are you loving your morning cup of coffee? Are you loving your car? Are you loving your hair? Are you loving your life???

One of the most important things we can do for ourselves is have appreciation for every little thing in our life. I am going to take you more through that process.

I will break it down into life situations throughout the book so that it just becomes natural for you to start looking at your life in a loving way—in all areas.

Let's face it...you are either loving it or you are hating it. Either way, it is taking up your energy. So, would you rather spend your energy in a loving way versus a non-loving way?

Everything is energy, right? Including love and hate. Where do we want to spend our energy? In love or hate? Listen, I have been there. I know what hatred feels like. I spent more time than I care to admit or remember, and it showed up everywhere on me physically. I looked older. I felt terrible. It showed up in every area of my life...the negativity in the bad vibes and the bad energy around that. So, I made a conscious decision that I didn't want to live that way anymore.

I am being as honest as I can when speaking about myself here. I'm hoping that this resonates with you, because let's face it, when we dig deep like this and we're honest, it isn't always pretty. We all need to uncover and find out where hatred is living in us.

Are you still holding on to anger and rage from betrayals you have been through or from people that have disappointed you? Is that serving you in your life today? Is that still showing up in any area of your life that could be, and let's face it, SHOULD be, in the past? Hatred and anger are just other forms of fear. So, what are you afraid of?

Why are we still carrying that old story around? Why are we still telling that story? Wouldn't you rather tell a better story about how loving you are and how much love you have to give, and how much love there is in the world? Isn't that a much better story?

We can look at the world and view all of its problems... or we can look at the world and see all of its beauty. It's just like that with ourselves; we can look at our world and see all of the problems... or we could look at our world and see how many gifts and blessings we have! We have SO much that we need to be grateful for!

Let's focus on where we can love ourselves more, and let's start simple. It doesn't have to be any grandiose thing. It could be as simple as "I love myself! I love me! When I look in the mirror I see love! I love my life! I love you! I love my kids! I love my body! I love my bed! I love my car! I love the sunshine!"

The list can go on and on and on. Doesn't that energy and that feeling feel way better inside of our bodies versus feeling negativity? Negative words and emotions feel dark, feel icky, and feel heavy. When you are focused on love, you feel lighter, you feel brighter, and you smile more!

Exercise:

Where in your life today do you want to feel better about loving? Whenever we are feeling down about ourselves, the quickest way to pick ourselves back up again is to reach out to somebody else and offer them our love. Maybe it's as simple as picking up the phone and calling somebody you haven't talked to in a long time, and saying to them "I'm thinking about you and I love you."

Giving is THE single best way you take the attention off of us and offer our love to someone else. It is uplifting, and it makes us feel good! That could be one easy thing you could do today…one simple step to make yourself feel even just one percent better about loving yourself and loving your life! So, let's start there…just one simple thing like that. Call someone.

In this chapter we learned:
• Love your life no matter what.
• Anger and hatred are forms of fear.
• Focus on all the positives.

For more information, go to www.dianeforster.com or www.ihavetoday.com. Enter your name and email address to become part of the "I Have Today" Community, and receive FREE gifts, like the "I Love You" Chant and the "I Forgive You" Chant.

THANK IT – EXPLAINED

Now, let's focus on "Thank It!" The fastest path to being in that "thankful" state is LANGUAGE. How are you speaking? What are the words that you are using when speaking to others? What is that voice going on and on about in your head? How are you talking to yourself? What are the words that you are saying about yourself and others?

Are they empowering thoughts or are they negative thoughts? Are they uplifting words or words that knock you down, bring you down, and keep you down?

Pay attention to your language and what you say. Do you say things like…I don't have, yeah but, I can't, it works for some people but not for me, etc.? Do you talk like that? Well, if you do, STOP IT! Words like that are so self-defeating.

How is your language related to money? Do you use words like debt, worry, and lack? These are all words that just disempower you. These types of words and language do not let you live your passion, your purpose, and your smile, your abundance and light! They keep you stuck and unhappy.

Let's do some work with gratitude and affirmations that is really going to switch the paradigm in your mind about the way your language is affecting your life, which is keeping you at a level you don't want to live on. I know you would rather live on a higher, more positive level. So, let's work on that.

Exercise:

Let's look at some examples of words and phrases you might be using that you could substitute with more positive words. Let's talk about the ways the language you are using could be affecting what is coming in and out of your life.

Let's start with "I just can't seem to get ahead". Instead, you might want to say "I am so thankful that things are always working out for me." You might be saying "I can't seem to get along with my partner." Instead you can say "I would love to find a new way to communicate better with my partner."

Can you see how that is more empowering? Can you see how that has more positive energy?

Another example could be "I just can't stand my job anymore." Instead, say "I am grateful for my job because it provides income for me." In saying it this new way, you are looking at it from a place of gratitude versus being ungrateful. (Remember...Thank It!)

Do you ever hear yourself saying something like this: "I don't have time to do the fun things that I like to do." Instead, say "I can make 'ME' time a priority, and I am going to calendar in an extra hour a week just for me! For me to do whatever is I want to do whether it is taking a bath, getting an extra hour sleep, going for a walk, getting a massage. Something that makes me feel GOOD!" Isn't that much more empowering?

I deeply connect with this one. I used to put myself on the bottom of the priority list. Everything else had to be done first. The house had to be clean, dishes had to be taking care of, the lunches had to be made, and the laundry needed to be done, the bills needed to be paid...and on and on. I realized there wasn't any time at the end of the day for me.

I learned to calendar in time for me, and I make it a priority every day. I set my alarm extra early in the morning so I have that quiet time for me. I carve out two full hours! I meditate, I write in my journal and then I exercise. I spend all that time doing what I should be doing. I nurture my spirit, I nurture my mind and I nurture my body. That is my daily practice, and that is my greatest gift from me to me.

It takes commitment. It is a commitment to myself, and once I started doing it, getting in the habit of it, now it is just second nature. It is time blocked off for me. It may not work for you; you may not be a morning person...but figure out the time of the day that is best for you.

Back to "Thank It" and language...be SO cognizant of the words you use! I have other products coming out to help with that, but for now, do your best to stay focused on gratitude. Feel free to send me your comments and feedback.

In this chapter we learned:
• Importance of using empowering and uplifting words.
• How to prioritize time for yourself.
• How to be more committed to yourself.

For more information, go to www.dianeforster.com or www.ihavetoday.com. Enter your name and email address to become part of the "I Have Today" Community, and receive FREE gifts, like the "I Love You" Chant and the "I Forgive You" Chant.

Bring It – Explained

"Bring It" is the final phase in the three-step process to gain your passion, purpose and smile...again or ever! This is when you take what you've experienced—the good, the bad, all of it and you move forward with your life in a more positive, powerful way because you are BETTER for the experiences you've had. They have made you clearer on who you are, what you do and don't want, and what you're willing to tolerate or not tolerate anymore. Also, since there are no wasted moments, you may not realize why certain events happened to you for a really long time. Just know that everything is always for our highest, greatest good. Always.

You now have the POWER to make better, more informed decisions, based on the fact that you have loved every experience, you thanked it for showing up in your life, and now...now you're better, smarter, wiser, more experienced, more enlightened and capable of knowing more clearly what you want! That is POWER baby!

Now you get to "Bring It" to all areas—in love, in money, in success, in relationships, in health and wellness—in every single area of your life!

Let's start breaking it down.

In this chapter we learned:
• What is 'Bring It?'
• How it all ties together.
• You have the power now to change the outcomes.

For more information, go to www.dianeforster.com or www.ihavetoday.com. Enter your name and email address to become part of the "I Have Today" Community, and receive FREE gifts, like the "I Love You" Chant and the "I Forgive You" Chant.

Bring It – Three Levels of Forgiving

One of the key ways to *really* start "Bringing It" and start loving your life is forgiveness. Forgiveness is huge! Forgiveness is so freeing for YOU.

Level 1: Forgiveness for you, for anything you have ever done or said in the past is critical! Let yourself off the hook already!

Level 2: Forgiveness of others releases *their* hold on *you*. When I learned how to forgive myself (which I still do every day, it is a practice believe me. New things come up all the time); it set me free. Know that this is a journey. This is a marathon…it is not a sprint.

When I learned the tools for how to forgive myself, it opened me up. It "lightened" me. It dropped hang-ups I had carried around for years! That was very, very empowering for me.

When I learned to forgive my ex, it was the most incredible, monumental thing I could do given the history that we had and the betrayal that was there…the lies and the distrust.

Because of my ability to forgive him, the circumstances, and the ability to forgive myself, we are now at a place where we have a very cohesive relationship. That is really important because we are connected to each other forever because of our children.

How he and I interact with each other deeply affects how our children react and respond, and how they interact with other people and carry on in their own relationships. They are well adjusted, and they have healthy relationships with both of us.

So…I can't tell you how important forgiveness is. It has such a ripple effect in our lives.

Level 3: Forgive yourself when old stuff bubbles up again. Even after you've done all of this work, there are times when old wounds come up. You think that chapter is closed and complete, but something may trigger it. That's the time that you need to forgive yourself AGAIN for the old feelings that have resurfaced. Just "love it" for showing up," thank it" for the reminder of how far you've come, and "bring it" by letting it empower you to release it again. Be easy, easy, easy on yourself!

NOTE: My "I Forgive You" Chant Process (just like the "I Love You" Chant) is the best tool I've ever used to create easy, effective, permanent forgiveness. You can find it on my website. Go there and download them. Let me know how it works for you!)

In this chapter we learned:
• Levels of forgiving.
• Forgiveness is so freeing.
• How to forgive ourselves.

BRING IT – INTEGRITY AND TRUST

Living a life of integrity and trust attracts positive people and relationships into your life...in all areas. Most of the delicate balance with communication in relationships is the importance of integrity and trust. You need to maintain your integrity and your truth...and do it in a polite way.

Speak your truth, but always come at it from HOW YOU FEEL. Speak authentically about the way you feel. It is all about you and your feelings, and not what someone does to you or says about you. You can't control others' actions. You can only control your reaction and response to it.

It is always based on your feelings. If you can remember that, you will keep the communication clean and authentic, which will then keep the communication open and respectful. That is how you'll be able to maintain healthy relationships with every single person in your life!

In this chapter we learned:
• Importance of trust in communication.
• Importance of speaking authentically about your feelings.
• Importance of keeping open communication.

BRING IT – INTUITION

Let's continue to bring it! This is your life. It is here; it is now! Remember…the name of the book is I HAVE TODAY! You owe it to yourself to do this work. This is YOU taking care of YOU. Part of our taking care of ourselves is looking at trusting our intuition. This was a big hurdle for me.

This took a lot of work…a lot of deep dive digging to where I didn't trust myself. There were too many times that something inside me didn't feel right, and it always happened when I didn't listen to my intuition. That played a huge role in where things went "wrong" in my life. It was me not listening to me, so I had to learn how to trust myself.

Are you having issues trusting yourself? Are you not listening to that little voice inside of you? It's a feeling inside of you that is telling you "something is just not right," "I am just not happy." or "this isn't the way I want to be, or live, or speak, or present myself."

I am going to tell you right now how I got back to trusting myself and my intuition. One of the things I did was start asking myself "Is this the right choice for me?" I will get very still and quiet, and if something doesn't feel right within my gut, right in the center of my body, then for me the answer is always a 'no." Whatever the situation is, I now say 'no' to it. The only way to say "yes" to something is if it feels good! It's literally that simple! How easy is that? This took me so long to figure out, but now I've got it mastered. It's not always easy to say no, but you have to care more about your well-being and your happiness more than you care about anything else. You come first…always.

So, where does your intuition "show up" in your body? Pay attention to it…and pay attention to the way you're feeling about things. TRUST it! That is your Inner Guidance System working on your behalf 24/7 in your life! It's never, ever wrong! It took me a long time to uncover that. But, now that I know, decisions in my life are so easy. We have one brain, but we have three minds: our head, our heart and our gut. Where in your body does your "mind" talk to you?

In this chapter we learned:
• Importance of listening to your intuition.
• Listening to yourself to bring your trust back.
• Say 'no' when you don't feel good about things.

BRING IT – COMMITMENT

How you are preparing for these changes in your life? You want to transform your life into a happier, passionate, purposeful life, right? You can do this really fast, but how are you going to prepare? How are you going to set yourself up to take action to really transform your life successfully?

What daily action steps are you prepared to take? Please don't go into this thinking it is going to just magically happen. It takes your commitment, and it takes daily action steps. They are not hard. None of this is going to be really hard, but it does take commitment, and it takes action by you.

I know this first hand, because I am taking action in my life. I am taking action right now, by sharing all of this with you, because I want to help you.

I have taken action in my life by taking leaps of faith.

I took action when I quit my corporate job, with no net underneath.

I took action when I sold my house with no place to live.

I took action when I moved cross country, not knowing how my life was going to unfold.

I took action when I created my first product. I invented something out of nothing, never doing anything like that before! I didn't know where this road was going to take me, but I went down it. It led me to being on QVC!

I encourage you to please live in action! Take a chance, open the door, make that leap, take this step to better your life because I am an example of how doors open and how there is unlimited opportunity for you! In order to get there, you have to take the first step, you have to take action, and you have got to get out of your comfort zone.

It is going to be a little uncomfortable. It is going to feel a little weird inside...but that is how we grow! If we are comfortable and we are sitting back hiding behind a veil (whatever your veil is), then you are not growing. Everything is energy, and everything is moving, so, if you are not growing, you are dying. It's just that simple...it's a universal law.

So, do you want to be living, or do you want to be dying? There are NO mistakes really...only lessons. Let me tell you how many mistakes I made during the invention process! Many, many, many! But, they were all valuable lessons!

There were mistakes all along the way during my QVC appearance. Most people wouldn't have noticed, but I did. However, my philosophy is everything is a work in progress and we just get better, and better, and better at it.

So, the next time I appear on air, I will be more experienced and prepared. That just makes me better prepared for the   next opportunity in general. You can't keep studying life, and you can't keep holding on to fear, doubt, and insecurity. You just have to do it! Jump out there!

Take the lead in your life. I have made many mistakes along the path in my life. For instance, let's look at parenting. As parents, how many mistakes do we make a day? A dozen a day, who knows! Yet we do a hundred things right and we tend to focus on the things we do wrong. Why is that?!

It's just all part of the process. This goes back to forgiveness too. We all need to work on that constantly. Trust me, we all need to be forgiving ourselves over and over and over again. So, just start...start taking action, know they'll be bumps and mistakes. It's ok, it's all forgivable, and you deserve to live the happy, purposeful, passionate life you want to live and not be afraid of it!

Now, everything I learned on this journey is all about momentum. You just have to start somewhere, and the key is you have to keep the momentum going.

You can start small, maybe do one little thing every day. But build on that and take the next step, then the next step, and so on. I learned that in my life with my business, my product business.

I came up with the idea for The Spifter out of a frustration in the kitchen one day. When you first come up with product ideas (it tends to happen with a lot of inventors), you have a lot of momentum in the beginning. You are excited about the idea, so you are busy in the creation process, following a sequence of steps. For me, I was just following along towards the next step, then the next step. Get a patent, create the business, get the drawings done, find a prototype manufacturer and get the prototype made, do market research, start making sales calls to see if anybody would want this product. The momentum just builds.

However, back then, my life was busy and very full. Working and raising my twins came first. I would stop and stall all of that because of the more important, pressing needs in my life. I wasn't fully committed to the passion of my product and my vision at the time. I was playing it safe and playing it small, and that was hurting my momentum. The momentum would fizzle. Please don't misunderstand. I was doing exactly what I wanted to be doing...being a mom to my beautiful children that I worked so hard to have. Raising them has been the greatest experience in my life, and I wouldn't change a moment of it for anything!

So, when the time was right, I planned out my course of action. Through commitment and through momentum, I got where I am today. I planned out a course for my life and I do what I can to stay committed to it. I got the momentum going where I was able to quit my corporate job. Talk about a leap of faith! I had two kids who just graduated high school and were heading off to college. How crazy, right? Who does something like that?!

I was committed to this entrepreneurship and committed to building my businesses. I am committed to doing this for me and creating the kind of life that I want to live. By doing so, I am setting an example for my kids that they can be or do or have anything! They can if they are committed and keep going! Keep the momentum moving forward!

I got the momentum going and it was step by step, by step. Right now in my life, in this year, at this time, I made a commitment to me that this year is all about me. This year is about building my businesses to a level that I can't even see.

I have no ceiling, it just doesn't exist. I set my sights really, really high. Since I opened that door and made that commitment out loud and affirm that this is the year of me, this is the year my businesses, there have been door, after door, after door of opportunities opening up for me. There have been so many resources, people, events, circumstances, you name it, magnetically appearing before me. It's incredible. I have an amazing team built all around me now and everybody is focused on my passion, my purpose, and what it is I want to do. They all share my mission and my vision. Now, that makes me smile!

The vision is bringing products and services to the world. I am creating a business and an empire that revolves around helping and supporting women. Not just emotionally and in personal development, but in the kitchen and lifestyle. I am not unique. ANYONE can do what I'm doing! You can do it too! All it takes is an idea, then commitment, and getting the momentum going. It really is that simple! Idea, commitment, momentum.

So, what small steps could you take right now that could move you in a new direction? Because you always want to be moving forward; you always want to be taking a step forward. Could it be committing to eating better? Committed to reading more, studying more, learning more? Committed to spending more time with your family...focused, fun, high quality time with your family?

Could you be committed to changing your "bubble?" Who is in your core circle right now? Who are the people around you? Sum up the five closest people around you...who are those people? Are those people elevating you and taking you to where you want to go and expanding you in any way? Or is this a comfort zone for you?

Are you the "shining star" in that circle, because if you are that one, then you are not growing and expanding, and you need to raise your game. You should surround yourself with people who are going to empower you, impassion you, enlighten you, lift you up and challenge you. You want to be stretching yourself in your business development or even just in your personal development.

It could be in any area of your life, but I definitely encourage you to build momentum in this area of your life as well. You want to be growing bit, by bit, by bit and your "tribe" has a lot to do with that.

Exercise:

Challenge yourself to add one new thing to your life this week. Then look back at the week to see what's changed. Where can you do more, where was it easy to make that shift, or where do you want to improve more? Just keep building momentum and keep the engine running. Keep the train moving forward. Keep going! That is what I do every day.

I say to myself every day, "How am I going to show up today? How can I serve? How I am going to grow and expand?"

And then I look back because I really don't know the answers going in. I think that is a beautiful thing! I have gotten really comfortable with uncertainty, which is why I love to write in my journal. That way, I can look back…look back on the day, look back on the week and say, "Look at all that has happened this week! I have really grown, I really moved forward, I am shifted. I have expanded, and that feels really good!"

So, I am encouraging you to do that for yourself.

In this chapter we learned:
• Are you prepared for commitment?
• Identifying ways to build momentum.
• Importance of challenging yourself for growth.

Bring It – Self Worth

I used to have this negative chatter in my mind all the time. I am not smart enough, I am not good enough, I am not worthy enough, I am not pretty enough, I am not thin enough. You know the wheel, the wheel that keeps going on and on.

You hear the chatter inside your head, over your shoulder, nagging like the annoying pain in the neck that it is! The best way to combat that never-ending dialogue is through positive affirmations and mantras. So...I made another commitment to myself. I committed that every day when I wake up, after my feet hit the floor, I say, "I love my life, I love my life, I love my life! Thank you, thank you, and thank you!"

I do and say things in threes because I believe it anchors it into my soul by telling it to my mind, my body and my spirit. Next, I go into the bathroom, I look in the mirror, and I say, "I love you, Diane. I am beautiful. I am worthy. I am smart. I am grateful. I am the best." Simple, yet very powerful words! There is so much written about daily words of affirmation and positive mantras. My particular routine is a culmination of all the wonderful teachings I've experienced in my life thus far.

I learn more and more every day. I'll get on this gratitude rampage that just lifts me up so I start my day with this massive burst of energy, which really helps alleviate that negative talk. I still have the negative talk; as long as we have egos, we will. It still can creep in there, but now I catch it immediately and I turn it around and say something positive.

I encourage you to start paying attention to what are you saying to yourself. What are the negative things that you are saying? If you do something and say "God, I am so stupid!"...that has a negative impact on you. Take the opportunity to turn it around and say, "I forgive myself because we all make mistakes. It's not a big deal. Did it really hurt anyone? Did it really hurt me or affect me?" Try using those kinder words and move on.

Exercise:

Remember, your life is right now, in this moment. I HAVE TODAY. The past is in the past, you are here today, right here, right now. Stay present, and maybe that should be your mantra that you start with. Try this: when something negative comes in, just say "I have today, I am doing okay! It is all good, and I'm moving in the right direction."

Catch yourself in those moments when you have that negative talk, and flip it around and switch it into something positive.

In this chapter we learned:
• Importance of encouraging to say good things to yourself.
• Why repeat things three times?
• Concentrate not on the past but today.

For more information, go to www.dianeforster.com or www.ihavetoday.com. Enter your name and email address to become part of the "I Have Today" Community, and receive FREE gifts, like the "I Love You" Chant and the "I Forgive You" Chant.

BOMBS – EED EMOTIONAL ENERGY DIFFUSER

EED stands for Emotional Energy Diffuser. The way it works is if you are trying to avoid some conflict, situation or confrontation that you don't want to get involved in, you would use this method. This stuff is good!

This is a three-step process that involves breathing, thinking, and praising. Here is how it works. The very first thing you do is just pause for a moment and take a breath. Deep inhale, then exhale. Breathing has a natural way of just calming ourselves down. Remember this...you are always only a breath away from feeling better. So, take a breath before saying or doing anything. Just a nice and easy breath.

The next step is to think. The only thing I want you to think about is this statement: "This has nothing to do with me." Because the truth is...it really doesn't! Whatever is going on with the other person has everything to do with them and has nothing to do with you! You have a choice in that moment to not react to what's going on, by remembering and acknowledging that this has nothing to do with you. It's never about you, it's always about what's going on with them. That's SO empowering!

The last step is praise the person in front of you. That's right. Offer them love and unconditional acceptance and say to yourself, "They are doing the best they can from where they are right now." Because they really are! You don't know what is going on with them or why they are reacting the way they are. Maybe they were having a bad day. Who knows? We all see things through our own eyes and have our own perspectives. No two people see things the same way. So, once you get that, it all comes down to practicing peace, understanding and compassion. That's how God sees us...never with judgement and always perfection. If you can implement EEDs into your life, I guarantee you are going to be much, much happier!!!

Remember: Breathe, Think, Praise.

In this chapter we learned:
• What EED stands for.
• Three-step process that involves breathing, thinking, and praising.
• Remember it has nothing to do with you.

For more information, go to www.dianeforster.com or www.ihavetoday.com. Enter your name and email address to become part of the "I Have Today" Community, and receive FREE gifts, like the "I Love You" Chant and the "I Forgive You" Chant.

EED PROCESS

Try as quickly as possible to remember and implement this process: Breathe, Think, Praise.

Here's something that I know for sure...whenever a situation arises in my life where I implement this practice, I know that wherever the other person is coming from is a place of unhappiness. They are either feeling unloved, unappreciated, not valued, not heard, feeling wronged, and so on. They are feeling "less than." And nobody wants to ever feel like that. We all want to be uplifted, to be seen and heard, to be valued, and to be loved, loved, loved!

Therefore, if you can remember that (which isn't easy...believe me. This took a very long time for me to figure it out, and I still have my moments where I forget), then the process will start to become easier. When you see just how fast it works, your "confrontations" will start to become "conversations." MUCH more productive. You'll be able to address the other person's *feelings*...not their *actions*. That is huge!

In this chapter we learned:
• Importance of remembering three-step process.
• Experience fewer bombs each day.
• It is about feelings, not actions.

Bombs – FEAR

One of our biggest bombs is fear! Fear shows up in a lot of different ways. It's like a big onion that we have to peel back the layers—all of our fears, doubts, insecurities, etc. Everything that we ever feel is either based on love or based on fear. Anything that is not love is really some other name for what is ultimately fear.

One of the biggest fears I had to overcome was when my marriage ended. After being with someone for over twenty years, I had to be on my own again. I hadn't done that since I was in my early twenties. I had no idea what that was going to look like. There was fear of being alone, fear of dating, fear of being a part-time parent, fear of money and stability. So many fears.

I love my kids so much, and only having them part-time was something that was very difficult for me to wrap my mind around. What did I do? I worked through them and realized that I have got to face my fears head on. I had to master a way to do that. Just like before, it's a three-step process. First of all, I take a deep breath. Breathing is how you know you're alive. Deep breathing (as in the Rainbow Breath Meditation Series) allows you to oxygenate your body, sending healing energy throughout…it calms your mind, and you instantly feel relief. Again, I keep repeating this, but we are always a breath away from feeling better.

Next: Think! " What's going on inside of me? I'm feeling fears and I need to get them out of me! I have got to vocalize them and express them." By doing that aloud, I was able to get them out of me physically.

Once we address what is holding us inside and release it out, we no longer carry it inside of us. It's releasing its hold on us. Not only did I verbalize them aloud, I practiced writing them down as well.

"I am afraid to be alone, I am afraid I won't be able to support myself, I am afraid my friends and family will judge me, I am afraid that my kids won't love me as much anymore, I am afraid I won't be able to ever be in a healthy relationship again, I am afraid to take chances." Do any of these resonate with you?

I worked hard to get rid of all of that stuff that was inside of me. What I found in the process was as time went on, I would clear away some fears, and another one would bubble up. So, I'd work through to clear that fear, and then another would bubble up. They don't ever fully go away, but...

Last: Praise! Until slowly but surely, I realized that you can feel fear; it is okay. It is "normal" to feel fear, but then it is okay to release it and let it go. It's ok to cut the ties with the fears, release yourself from the contract with it, because it is no longer serving me or anyone else! So, I praise the fear and show gratitude by saying, "Thank you, fear, for showing up. Now I release you. I get rid of this, and it is done! I am OK! And I always will be OK!"

Breathe deeply, acknowledge the fears, verbalize them and write them out, know it's OK to feel the fear, and then it's OK to cut the ties and release it...just let it go! That is the way to diffuse fear bombs.

Remember: Breathe, Think, Praise.

In this chapter we learned:
• Discovering our fears.
• How to face fears.
• How to get rid of fears.

For more information, go to www.dianeforster.com or www.ihavetoday.com. Enter your name and email address to become part of the "I Have Today" Community, and receive FREE gifts, like the "I Love You" Chant and the "I Forgive You" Chant

BOMBS – ANXIETY

The anxiety bomb is also a big bomb. You are anxious, you've got a lot going on, a million things going on all at once. You're hustling to make the kids' lunches and to get out the door so they can get to school on time, you are rushing to get to work, or you are late for a meeting, etc. Whatever the scenario is, it makes us feel anxious.

We all know that feeling so well. It just seems to keep perpetuating, and it builds and builds and builds. It seems like the more you are lost in that state, the bigger the bomb gets.

A very effective technique that I use to diffuse those bombs is, that's right, the three step process.

First Step…Breathe! Remember, you are always a breath away from feeling some relief. I can't say that enough. That will always make you feel better and allow you to pause and think for a second.

Next Step…Think! Ask yourself "What am I doing? Do I want to be in this space, feeling this way, could I be feeling better, could I be doing something differently, is this as bad as I think it is?" Uh….no! It never is!

Now comes the last step…Praise! Say to yourself "All is well! Things are going to be okay!" Acknowledge that things really are going to be okay, and then allow yourself to just slowly ease back into whatever it is you are doing from a calmer and more relaxed state. Then, just like that, you will diffuse the bomb instantly. I promise you, these practices are as easy as one, two, three. And they work!

Just like I said, they are easy as one, two, three but it takes time and habit. It takes your commitment, and it takes your momentum. Here is how I diffused the anxiety bomb recently.

Funny Story:

I was running late, which I try not to be. (I really do try to be on time...although stuff happens sometimes. Yeah, yeah...I know. Listen, I am work-in-progress, and there will always be room for improvement with me.)

I was on my way out to a meeting, and I had several things on my agenda to do that afternoon. I wanted to make sure I didn't forget anything in the house on my way out the door. So, I had a pile of things by the front door, ready to go with me. I would go to the post office, I would go to the cleaners, I would go to my meeting, and I had some things to do at the bank and some other various everyday errands.

As I was trying to get out the door phone rang. I was multitasking as it is (by the way, there's no such thing as multi-tasking...that's an illusion, and I'll write more on that on another day.) I was doing what we women do, which is taking on more than we should all at once. I had my purse on my shoulder, my briefcase in my hand, the phone to my ear held by my hand, and I bent over and tried to scoop up everything that I had piled on the floor. As I picked up everything and turned towards the door, I walked right into the door and everything in my hands went crashing to the floor! The water bottle that I had hit the floor and cracked open...and spilled water all over the mail I was bringing to the post office. There was paper and water everywhere. Now, I could have really lost it in that moment.

Instead, I politely hung up the phone and stopped for a minute. I took a deep breath, and the truth is I just burst out laughing and I thought to myself, "Who does this? Who tries to manage this many things like this all at once?" It was a very funny, comical moment.

My next thought was "Everything is okay. Diane, it is okay if it takes an extra minute to get out the door. Everything is going to be just fine!"

We put these pressures on ourselves to overdo, to over commit, and over perform. We are our hardest critics on ourselves, and we don't need to be like that. Do you know why? It's because it is not that hard! Life REALLY is supposed to be easier than this; it IS supposed to be more fun! Seriously!

I took that moment to acknowledge that, to recognize the comedy of it all, and to put a big smile on my face. Through my laughter, I picked up and dried off my mail, I put my water bottle in the recycle bin, and I picked up everything else that I had on the floor. I then slowly walked to my car, loaded everything into it and went off with my day. Everything was fine, and actually the rest of the day went along really well and smoothly. It was all because I took that brief moment to diffuse what could have turned into a bad situation for me.

I encourage you to take on these action steps as well. Just take on those three steps if you are in a situation similar to this. Just know that life really isn't as difficult as we make it out to be, and having a process to turn to definitely makes those tough moments much more palatable.

Momentum is momentum. You can feel bad momentum just like you feel good momentum. You can tell as anxiety is building…you know when it's coming. You start to feel the pressure, and it is like a pressure cooker.

You know when it is coming on, and you know you have been there before when it doesn't end well.

It ends up being like the situation I just described. So, try to catch yourself early on. The more we do this, the easier it will get. You'll get to the point where you are just cruising through your days. You are just flying through them. They are easy, they are effortless, and you are living your life with purpose, with your passion, and with your smile.

Remember: Breathe, Think, Praise.

In this chapter we learned:
• Three-step technique to defuse anxiety bomb.
• Acknowledging anxiety and handling hard situations.
• Controlling anxiety.

BOMBS – WORRY

Bomb number three: worry. This is a big problem that needs to be diffused. Okay, throughout my life experiences I have come to know this…that worry is a wasted emotion. Let me repeat that…WORRY IS A WASTED EMOTION! If you think about all the time in your life that you spent worrying about things, then think about how many of those things actually came true, to fruition. I am going to venture to say that probably none to very, very few, right? So then, why do we spend so much of our time worrying? What is that? That is something that needs to be diffused permanently and to get rid of! You just need to rid worry right out of your life!

Let's use the three-step process with worries as well.

Remember: Breathe…because that makes you feel better, right?

Then, Think. You'll want to say yourself, "Is this something that I really need to be worried about?"

Last, the third step is to praise. Praise God, praise whomever or whatever you believe in, that everything happens in divine timing and order. I mean, truly, ask yourself, "Do I have any real control over this situation anyway?" I'm guessing the answer to that is a resounding NO.

For example, my daughter was in a car accident, and I was hundreds of miles away from her---nowhere near where she was. I couldn't get to her if I wanted to, and there was nothing I could do about it. Fortunately and thank God, she was fine. Her car was rear ended. Although she and her friend were fine, there was a lot of damage to the car. It was not drivable, and she couldn't get ahold of me.

That is a parent's worst nightmare, right? We keep our phones next to us at all times. Even if we are not able to be in communication at all times, we keep them close by "just in case something happens."

71

Well, guess what...that something happened, and my phone was nowhere near me. I was upstairs, and my phone was downstairs charging.

So, what happened...she couldn't get a hold at me, and she handled every detail all the way around on her own. She called AAA, the tow truck came out and took her to the nearest body shop. Then, she went across the street to rent a car. About 45 minutes after the accident, I saw all the missed calls and thought "Oh My God...what's going on?" That was the first thing that crossed my mind.

As she explained everything to me, I could not have been more proud of her! That girl took control of everything! She handled the whole situation on her own without me. That is, for me, a parents' greatest wish—independent, self-sufficient children/adults! So many of us parents think our kids can't function without us. What if something happens? What if I am not there?

The truth of the matter is...even if you are there, it is out of your hands. You can't control it; they are the ones that are in control of their lives. You can only control what is going on with you.

So, don't worry about it. Give them back their lives. Trust that you are giving your kids the skills and the tools they need to be out in the real world to manage things themselves. My daughter handled that and executed it perfectly. I couldn't have told her anything better to do, or have done anything differently than she did on her own. That gave me such peace of mind.

My son has always been so independent. If the situation had happened to him, I would expect the same exact outcome. I feel so blessed to be their mom. They make me so proud every single day!

I believe that I removed worry from my life through this process. There is very little, if anything, that ever really worries me. If a worried thought comes in, I do my best to diffuse it right away. Let me tell you that I have a much more peaceful life from that perspective because of it.

Could I have done anything differently? No! Would I have done anything differently? No! Was there anything to worry about? No!

As a parent, is there any better scenario than your kids taking care of things on their own? I don't think so.

As a mother, that is one of my proudest moments. I thought, "Thank you God, thank you for letting me see my daughter in action as a grown independent woman handling things on her own. She is eighteen years old, and she has got it handled!"

That is my wish for you, for your children, and your parenting. Release your worry. They have got it handled; they are paying attention. The best way to teach is by example.

If you set an example of a worrier, you will create a worrier. However, if you set an example of someone who is living in peace, following your truths, going through your day-to-day life with passion and purpose and a smile on your face, you will have kids who also have passion, purpose, and a smile on their face!

That is how you serve your children. Get rid of the worry; you don't need it. It is not serving you. And comfortably put that smile back on your face!

In this chapter we learned:
• That worry is a wasted emotion.
• It is all out of your control.
• How to get rid of worries.

For more information, go to www.dianeforster.com
or www.ihavetoday.com. Enter your name and email address to
become part of the "I Have Today" Community, and receive
FREE gifts, like the "I Love You" Chant and the "I Forgive
You" Chant.

DEFINING YOU

Let's define you. Let's talk about bringing your sexy back, because we all have a sexy goddess in us. Let's reignite her, and bring her to life!

Perhaps you're an 'empty nester' and playing the role of mom has been a big part of your life, but you haven't had that feeling of being a sexy or powerful woman in a really long time, if ever. Or...you might be someone who is divorced and you want to get back in touch with that sexy feminine side of you.

I am encouraging you immediately, right away, top of the list, get your sexy back! It feels SO GOOD! I got mine back, and I "rock it" as much as possible! I don't care how egotistical that sounds! All I know is I feel more alive than I ever have!

One of the best and easiest ways to bring your sexy back is to go on a lingerie shopping spree. Go through that underwear draw of yours, and get rid of all those old cotton, torn, unmatched sets! Just toss all that stuff in the trash! Get rid of those torn, worn out bras! I know you have them in there, because I did too. I also know that many of you have a drawer full of this stuff and you wear the same three bras all the time. Am I right, or am I right?

Getting rid of that old stuff leaves space physically and metaphorically, for new things. I encourage you to go and buy some fun pieces. Your size is irrelevant. YOU ARE SO BEAUTIFUL! This is about YOU. You are doing this for you! Others may benefit, but at the end of the day, it's all about how you want to feel. You. So empowering.

Another way to bring your sexy back is to plan a night to go out on the town. A night to dress up, go out with either your partner or with girlfriends, but just go! Part of dressing up is wearing something you feel amazing in...like an LBD. If you don't own one, get one. Every woman should own a little black dress, one that makes you feel stunning whenever you wear it.

Another one of the many ways to bring your sexy back is to go buy yourself a pair of sexy high heels. I tell you, I had the same conservative, low heeled, comfortable shoes that I wore all the years I worked. On the weekends and my days off, I wore sneakers or flats as I ran around town. Boringgggg! This is the fun part. Who doesn't love going shoe shopping?

So do it. Go out and buy yourself a sexy pair of heels. Something that you normally wouldn't buy, but when you have them on, they showcase your legs so they look long and lean, so sexy and beautiful. Make sure you love the way they look on your feet. Feel good in them!

Now you have your Power Outfit—you've got your sexy lingerie, you've got that little black dress and your hot new heels! You are going out on the town and you are feeling beautiful. No one will be able to take your eyes off of you!

When you go out, make sure to be in a place where as many people as possible can see you. Just take it all in and allow yourself to love the way that feels--being looked at and admired. Being the center of attention. Exude complete confidence!

That experience will ignite the sexy in you, and you will feel amazing, I promise you! Talk about feeling passion, and purpose, and smiling. You will be smiling from ear to ear! I want you to send me your pictures of your sexy outfit, your power look. I would love to see them!

In this chapter we learned:
• How to bring your sexy back?
• Go on a fun shopping spree all for you!
• Get out there and exude confidence.

For more information, go to www.dianeforster.com or www.ihavetoday.com. Enter your name and email address to become part of the "I Have Today" Community, and receive FREE gifts, like the "I Love You" Chant and the "I Forgive You" Chant.

HOW ARE YOUR SHOWING UP?

How are you showing up in your life? Are you giving it a hundred percent? Are you living intentionally in every moment? Or, are you just dragging your way through the day? This is YOUR day, YOUR life. I mean…it is today, it is right now, this is your life right now, so how do you want to live it? Do you want to live it halfway or do you want to live it all the way?

It is really important to ask yourself that question because how you show up affects everything in your life. It took some major life lessons, but I figured out that I really want to show up big!

Believe me, I showed up many days halfway and many days way less than half way. Now, I live my life with full intention, knowing that life is NOW; it's not yesterday or tomorrow. It's right now, and I don't want to waste a moment of this precious life! There is a process called segment intending and I do my best to practice it all day, every day. It basically means that you set intentions for whatever you're doing, wherever you're going, etc. When I wake up, I intend to make this a magical day, I intend to enjoy a delicious cup of coffee, I intend to be open to any new possibilities, and I intend to embrace the uncertainty that comes with each new day, and so on. I do my best to go through each and every step of each day in a positive way.

That is how I live my days…very, very intentionally. When you show up a hundred percent, you can't help but contribute a positive effect in all the areas of your life, and on other people. That energy is so magnetic, you'll just attract so many positive people, events, and experiences into your life. It's magic!

I encourage you to show up in your life with all of your passion, and purpose, and smile that you can master up, show up at one hundred percent. Living intentionally (in addition to of all the other topics discussed) builds momentum. Positive momentum like this continues to snowball into happiness, fulfillment, enjoyment, peace—you name it. All the qualities we say we want in life. Well, as you follow my process, all of that can be yours too!

It is about continuing that motion forward and keeping it going. Easy, simple steps. Layer upon layer. These are all very easy but effective steps to create a powerful life for you—an enriched life, one full of passion, purpose, that keeps you happy and smiling. That is what I want for you!

I would love to know if this changes the way that you are showing up in your life and what the effects have been for you. If you start to notice a pattern of your days getting better, and better, and better, please share that with me.

In this chapter we learned:
• How are you showing up in your life?
• Live with intention.
• How to create powerful life for you.

COMMUNICATION WITHOUT EMOTION

Is it possible to have communication without getting emotional? Yes, it is. I know this is a big issue because most of our communication involves emotion, right? So, how is it even possible?

When we are communicating with other people we have emotions, because typically we want to express our feelings about something. There is a way to do this that can be very cohesive and calm, that can effectively communicate your unique styles together, back and forth, in a way where everyone can be heard, respected, and understood.

One of the things I needed to do for myself was to take a step back and look at myself. I would hear from others on occasion, "Why you are responding like that? Why do you have to be so terse?" I had no idea that I was coming across that way. The truth is that we don't really see ourselves. Most of the time, if not all the time, we can't really see what we look like, or hear what we sound like.

I wasn't even aware that I was giving off this harsh, terse, negative response to things. (I just chalked it up to my New York accent.) I'm sure part of the reason was I just had other things going on in my mind. So, in all fairness, I probably wasn't fully present in the conversation.

People perceived that I didn't care, that I wasn't really interested. That's not what was going on, but I realized that I needed to do something about that perception. That's when I decided to stop, take a step back, and really look at myself first and become "aware."

Do you know how you are coming across to others? Are you present, are you listening intently to the person? Do you recognize any patterns and perceptions that you don't feel are congruent with who you are?

Are you fully giving the person you're with the space, the eye contact, the respect they desire and deserve, that "100% audience"...completely present in that moment? Being aware of this will not only help them to feel heard and acknowledged, but it also helps you—you'll feel the effects of being appreciated for your listening skills.

Another tool I would suggest is called a mirroring technique. This has been around for years, so some people may be familiar with it. Mirroring basically means you mirror back what the other person says to you in order to let them know you heard exactly what they said. For example, if someone said to you something like "When you talk on the phone when I am in the room while I am trying to watch TV, it really irritates me because I can't hear the TV. That's so selfish, and I really wish you wouldn't do it."

Some of us might react with, "Well, this was a really important phone call that I needed to take, and the cell reception only works in this room. Why can't you go watch TV in another room?"

Does any of that sound vaguely familiar? Does conversation that starts out this way have any chance of ending with good feelings? Doubtful, right?

A better, healthier way to respond to that conversation would be, "What I just heard you say is that you have a hard time hearing the TV when I am on the phone in the room because I am talking loudly, which is disrupting the experience you are having with the TV program you are watching." The typical response would be, "Yes, that is what I said."

Now, that creates an opportunity for the response to be something equally calm and peaceful. "I understand, and I respect that. I needed to have that conversation in that room at that time because that is where the cell reception is the best in the house, and it was a very important phone call. So, I apologize if my phone call disturbed you. How about the next time I am expecting an important phone call, I will let you know ahead of time so that you have the opportunity to go watch TV in the other room. Would that work?"

Done! Diffused, simple, easy, calm, peaceful.

Another example of communication with peace is politely removing yourself away from "toxic" conversations. Let's say you are in a social setting with your girlfriends. Everything is going along fine, and then it turns into a bitch session or gossip session. The conversation just starts getting more and more negative. I found that I don't like to be in those environments because, for me, that is not healthy and it no longer aligns with who I am. I would much rather spend my energy talking about positive and uplifting things. This isn't judgment…this is just what works for me.

So, how do I delicately handle situations like that? What I try to do is politely excuse myself from the conversation if possible and go join in on a different conversation going on.

If you are in a smaller, more intimate setting with friends, and there is nowhere to go, politely try to veer the conversation in a different direction or a new topic. If that doesn't work, simply say, "If you don't mind, I am going to stay out of this conversation. I just don't want to engage."

By owning your values and respecting your boundaries, you will tend to see that response diffuses the negative conversation. Without being accusatory or pointing fingers, all of a sudden the others in the group have a heightened awareness of what's taking place, and now, they no longer want to participate in that kind of talk. It self-corrects the situation in a way that is very peaceful. I find that is really an effective way to keep the communication with peace going in a social setting like that.

These are just a few examples of ways to communicate without letting our emotions get in the way. That leads to more peace in your life. The less drama in your life, the more room for fulfillment of passion and purpose.

In this chapter we learned:
• Communication without emotions.
• How to make sure we are communicating peacefully.
• Escaping politely if you don't want to engage.

EMPOWERING YOU

This is so important. Empowerment means everything. We tend to take the back seat by putting everybody else's needs in front of our own. Then, we inevitably get lost in the mix. We want so much to please everyone, and the squeaky wheel always gets the grease. By doing so much for others as opposed to putting ourselves first, we wind up feeling depleted, drained, and exhausted...which is very far away from feeling our strength and power.

With all of that depletion comes the self-defeating negative conversations with ourselves. Why do we talk about ourselves this way? We are divine, amazing, wonderful beings. But we say things to ourselves like we are not smart enough, we are not good enough, we are not pretty enough, we are not deserving enough, we are fat, we are ugly, we will never lose this weight, we will never have time to do the things we want to do. We can go on, and on, and on. We have to stop it!

Our self-dialogue, whether spoken aloud or even just to ourselves, is having a ripple effect on everyone around us...especially on our children. They learn by example. They watch what we do and they mirror us. They can't help it.

So, it's incumbent on you to empower yourself with empowering words...words like I am worthy, I am a goddess, I am divine. Affirm over and over, and over again every day until you believe it!

Another element to connecting with your power is by creating healthy boundaries. One way to do that is by getting comfortable saying the word "no" to people. There are many ways to say "no" in a very healthy way to all of the people in your life without causing negative feelings or reactions. Talk about empowering kids with skills like that! They will learn that just by watching the example of you. Now, that's empowering!

A really effective way of empowering myself was using affirmations. Affirmations can be really powerful, but you have to use the right affirmations. If they don't resonate with you, then it's just empty airtime.

I have created a list of affirmations...very powerful affirmations. It's part of the LOVE IT! THANK IT! BRING IT! System. They are all designed to ignite the empowerment that lives within you. They build upon each other, creating lasting changes in your subconscious.

LOVE IT! – Affirmation Statements.

THANK IT! – Gratitude Statements.

BRING IT! – Power Statements.

For example:

LOVE IT! I AM SO EMPOWERED!

THANK IT! I AM SO GRATEFUL FOR MY EMPOWERMENT!

BRING IT! I HAVE ROCKET SHIP POWER!!!

Can you feel how strong those statements are? Say them aloud. Put some real power behind them when you say them.

I've spent a lot of time putting together really powerful affirmations. You can find them on my site. Pick the ones that resonate with you and serve you best. I have found the more I affirm, the more the empowerment flows to me and through me. It's good to "own" it and know who you are; what you're willing to do and not do; to be "selfish" in a good way (more on that later in the book.) It is not something to feel guilty about or bad about. You are not taking away from anybody else by you being selfish and putting yourself first and empowering you. You will actually be giving more!

By my doing this process, I have affected the lives of many, many women out there who have been inspired by my empowerment, and now, they are more empowered women themselves.

I can't say enough about the force of being an empowered person. It is your birth right. It is who you are. It is your essence. Do not discount that...don't play small! When you play small, you deprive this world of your greatness.

You have to play big. You have to shine bright. You have got to be the biggest, boldest, most wonderful being that you can possibly be...and that takes empowerment.

So, please, I encourage you, get the affirmations. Download them and use them. Then, let me know how they are working for you and where the shifts are happening in your life on your path to your passion, purpose, and never ending smile!

In this chapter we learned:
• Stop self-defeating negative conversations with ourselves.
• How to choose more empowering words.
• Power of affirmations.

What Are You Good At?

As you are on the road back to finding your purpose, and your passion, creating a smile back on your face, a key question is, "What am I good at?" Well...what are you good at? What are the things that you hear constantly from people that you are good at?

It could be cooking, it could be organizing, it could be running meetings, it could be head of the PTA, it could be soccer coaching, it could be knitting, painting, dancing, singing, playing an instrument, anything you feel that you are good at.

Take some time because this is important to know. The reason is because we want to marry up what you are good at with some other questions to find out what your true purpose may be.

One of the exercises I've done is I sent out an email to five of the closest people of my life—the people who know me the best. I asked them, "If you wouldn't mind, can you tell me what you think I am good at? What are my core values? What are my positive traits? What adjectives would you use to describe me? (This might feel a little uncomfortable for you, but I encourage you to do it because people DO like to help!)

Next, when you do get the feedback back from them, please call them and thank them. That is such a huge gift they just gave you! They have acknowledged you and your request, which is a beautiful thing.

Now, take those lists and combine them altogether. You will begin to see a pattern. Pick up the words and the descriptions of you that you see on that list and you will get a clear vision of what it is others think you are good at.

Lastly, compare that list to the thoughts and feelings you have about yourself. Do you see any similarities as to where your passions may be? This is an eye opening, fun exercise!

In this chapter we learned:
• Defining what we are good at.
• Asking others to support us defining our strengths.
• Analyzing feedback.

WHAT DO YOU LIKE TO DO?

Step One was figuring out what you are good at. Let's move on to Step Two.

Step Two is figuring out what it is you like to do. What do you enjoy doing? What are the things you do that allow time to pass quickly without even noticing it going by? Hours feel like minutes. Time loses all reality when you are involved in doing it. What are they? How far back can you remember? Go as far back as you can into your childhood and remember those activities. As a child, what did you love to do?

Did you love to color, build with Legos, play with Barbies, jump rope, play sports, swim, watch TV, play board games, crossword puzzles, etc.?

Go back to some of that playful stuff, and don't just make it all business related or work related things. Include those things too, like working with numbers or writing, etc. Don't leave anything out.

Get out a notebook and a pen and write out that list. Let yourself just go! Fill the page...in fact, fill two pages or more! Without over thinking it and allowing yourself to just flow, write as much as you possibly can about the things you really enjoy doing.

In this chapter we learned:
• Defining what we like to do.
• Make a list of what we like doing.
• Go back to playful stuff.

GET PAID TO DO WHAT YOU LOVE

Step Three. You now have the list of what you are good at and the list of things that you like to do. Now, the question you want to ask yourself is, "What can I do combining these lists that I can get paid for?"

Here is some guidance to help spark your creative juices. A perfect example is a friend of mine who loves photography. She likes to take pictures out in nature. Random pictures while she's out and about, at parks, the beach, wherever. She also loves animals and is a huge dog lover. She was feeling uninspired in her current job. She was looking for what her next adventure was going to be.

So, we put on our thinking caps together and asked the question, "How can she make a business out of using her skill as a photographer and her love of animals?" Answer: Take candid photos of owners with their pets out in public and sell them to the owners. How simple and easy is that!?! She created business cards for herself, a small little price list and she was open for business!

She walks around the parks (dog parks and public areas), which she's already doing with her own dog! She sees people interacting and playing with their dogs. She asks, "Would you mind if I took some pictures of you with your dog? And if you like them, I will send you the digital images for a small fee. This is a new business I've started and I'm building up my portfolio." Most people are more than happy to allow her to do that creating. The beauty is she catches people and their dogs in their natural element and their true essence.

Dog owners LOVE their dogs! Who doesn't love to get a picture of themselves with their dog? I mean, I know people who go to photography studios with their pets and have formal portraits done with them. Isn't this a great alternative?

This is just one example. There are so many ways to take the things that you are good at and then the things that you like to do and create a business around it. It is easy! It is fun! What a great exercise! Enjoy it!

This is my three-step process to help you dig in and find out what your purpose and your passion is to create a new level of growth in your life personally and professionally.

I am anxious, very anxious to hear how this process works for you and what ideas you have come up with and the ways that you can make this work for your life. Please email me your comments and your success stories, I want to know every one of them!

In this chapter we learned:
• Identifying what we are good at.
• Can we turn it to a business and being paid?
• Three-step process to find out your purpose.

For more information, go to www.dianeforster.com or www.ihavetoday.com. Enter your name and email address to become part of the "I Have Today" Community, and receive FREE gifts, like the "I Love You" Chant and the "I Forgive You" Chant.

YOUR RELATIONSHIPS

We touched on how you are "showing up" in your life. Now, let's break it down and get more specific—particularly in your romantic relationship. Whether it is a marriage or partnership, how are you showing up in that relationship? Even if you're not in a romantic relationship, you may desire one. If so, this is relevant in moving forward because how you showed up in your last relationship will definitely repeat itself if you don't look into your part of where the relationship fell apart. How did you "show up" there?

For those of you currently in a relationship, are you all in? Are you halfway in? Are you looking around for something better or are you committed to your partner? Are you keeping the communication and the dialogue open with this person?

We all know that relationships are work, but they are so worth it! The sharing of yourself with another is one of our greatest experiences on this earth. Know that the relationship will look different every single day! It's never the same from one to the next. One day, you love him, the next day, you can't stand him! That's so normal. If you understand that about relationships, it makes your life so much easier!

Is part of your passion and purpose in life to make this relationship work and be the best it can be? Loving and fulfilling. It is so easy for us to dismiss things and walk away. It takes much more effort to actually make a relationship work. So, ask yourself some questions:

How am I showing up for my partner? Am I being loving and supportive to him/her? Do I give to him/her first without expecting to get something from them? Am I open to receiving whatever it is they are capable of giving to me in any moment and being in gratitude and appreciation of that? These are some really great questions to ask yourself on a daily basis! Write them down on a piece of paper and put them somewhere you can see them every day.

How are you showing up in your sex life? Most of the time, is it him wanting it more than you and you finding reasons not to? What does your commitment look like in the boudoir department? Without question, sexual intimacy is the most vital part of any romantic relationship. It is the cornerstone of the relationship. It is way too important to show up to that halfway. Plus, it's so much fun! If your sex life isn't fun and something you both look forward to, that needs to be addressed immediately! One of the main reasons why women have no passion or purpose is because they are so unfulfilled in this area. Please reference the chapter on getting your sexy back to help you.

I'm not saying there's anything wrong with you...there's nothing wrong with you! Could your partner be doing more? Absolutely. Could he have treated you better, been more attentive, put your needs first at times? I'm sure the answer is yes. I just want YOU to have the richest, most fulfilling relationships you can with everyone in your life! Just ask yourself how you are showing up, could you be doing better, could you be doing more, what can you be doing better? When we give, we get. It just is. Giving feels good!

Explore that for a while and challenge yourself to step that up if you can. If you are not happy with a relationship or in a situation, that means there is a room for improvement, right? There's always room for love.

If you are teeter tottering on the fence about your relationship and are nearing throwing in the towel, give yourself the opportunity to explore working on the relationship one last time. Take the action steps of asking yourself all of those questions. Be the first one to apologize, be the initiator of sex. If that's not something you do normally, you will knock his socks off! He will not know what to do with himself! How much fun would that be!

So, when I say how you are "showing up" in relationships, now you know what I mean.

We are here on this planet to connect with people. Relationships are the main reason why we come into physical form. They fill us up and we can't take them for granted. We have to "show up" a hundred percent…for everyone, and especially ourselves!

In this chapter we learned:
• Relationships are worth it.
• How committed we are to the relationship we have.
• Importance of being an initiator sometimes.

For more information, go to www.dianeforster.com or www.ihavetoday.com. Enter your name and email address to become part of the "I Have Today" Community, and receive FREE gifts, like the "I Love You" Chant and the "I Forgive You" Chant.

IT's NOT PERSONAL

I love this question: how do you not take things personally? When someone says or does something directed towards us, we feel attacked, underappreciated, like a victim. Well, here's how not to. It's actually pretty easy. No one lives inside of us, right? We are all our own beings. We all have our own actions, our own minds, and our own way of expressing ourselves.

We are not mind readers, so we can't possibly know what is going on with somebody else. We can only know what is going on with ourselves.

The answer to how you not take it personally is that you CHOOSE NOT TO. What's going on with them has nothing to do with you! It's actually none of your business. You have no control. It's their experience. Even if someone is saying to you "You make me feel...when you..." that is still no reason to take it personally. That is the other person's experience. It's not yours.

My daughter and I are so alike in many ways. Translation: we either get along beautifully or it's as if we are speaking different languages. That's common, especially with mother/daughter relationships. I know I had a period of my life where it was that way with my mom and me.

When we are in that space, it's hard not to take it personally. It's hard to continue from a place of love and compassion. But, no matter what is going on with us, I didn't "do" anything to her or "make" her feel a certain way, just like she didn't "do" or "make" me feel anything either. We are both responsible for our own feelings. We both have our own perceptions of what happened in the situation. And you know what? We are both right. We are because that's our own truth. We each have our own defined emotions. Our emotions are our indicators of everything. However, no one can make us "feel" anything. We get to decide. It's always an inside job. It's not outside of us…ever!

When you understand this, your life becomes a whole heck of a lot easier. You stop "ingesting" other people's emotions. Remember the EED Process. This works beautifully here. Breathe, say "this has nothing to do with me," then praise the other person by saying in your mind, "they are doing the best they can from where they are." It's really to protect yourself from unwanted emotional energy and it diffuses whatever is transpiring faster. When you understand that the only person responsible for your happiness is you—no conditions, no outside people, no circumstances—you remember how valuable your emotional well-being is. You learn that taking things personally doesn't serve you. So, stop doing it! You'll thank me.

In this chapter we learned:
• What's going on with someone else has nothing to do with us.
• Realizing that we don't have to take on anyone else's energy.
• Your emotional well-being means everything.

Finding Your Sanctuary & Peace

As we continue to define you, a key process is finding your place of peace. Your sanctuary. An area just for you to be alone. As I've said before, I attribute my meditation practice to be the largest contributor to my massive shift. This sanctuary should give you peace of mind, which is so important to your overall state of emotional wellness. It could be a room in your house, or a section of a room where you could create an altar. It could be a bench in a beautiful park somewhere that you visit every day. My sanctuary has changed since I recently moved. All I do is sit on the couch in the living room, with my journal next to me on one side. I meditate every morning upon waking up, followed by writing in my journal. It sets the tone for the day, as I always start the day in a peaceful, calm place. It's so delicious.

Another one of my sanctuaries is the beach. I'm very lucky that I live at the beach, so when I have time, I go there. The beach is my heaven. This is the place I feel most at home. I am so connected to the water. I love the sound of the ocean, I love to feel the sand underneath my feet, I love watching the birds fly, I love seeing people walking on the beach, watching kids play, and feel the wind blowing through my hair. For me, it is just paradise. It's the perfect sanctuary!

It's like exercise; you need to put it in the calendar and block off time for it. I encourage you to do this daily.

This doesn't have to be anything that is long or drawn out. It's as simple as fifteen or twenty minutes, quietly breathing, with your eyes closed. I encourage you to do my Rainbow Meditation practice to keep you focused and the mind noise down.

Find where your sanctuary is and go to that space. Make that time a minimum of fifteen minutes a day, and cherish it. Don't skimp on yourself. You DO have the time! Everything else will get taken care of. It's about nurturing you. That is your time. That is your space. It's all for you.

In this chapter we learned:
• Sanctuary and your peace as a vital part to your overall state of emotional wellness.
• Importance of your morning meditation.
• Finding the place of your sanctuary and going to that place.

DEALING WITH THE EMPTY NEST

Hey all you "empty nesters"…now what do you do with all that time? I'll bet many of you have asked that question. If you've been caring for your children, which is the hardest job there is, but now the house is empty, you may be feeling lost. (And, some of you may be doing a happy dance!) What do you do with yourself now to fill your days?

This is a perfect time to evaluate what it is you want out of life. If you are feeling lost, if you are feeling like all you have done is raise kids and have nothing to contribute to the world, I am telling that you have far more skills than you think!

You have been running a home, which is what a project manager does. If you've raised children and seen them off to college, you deserve a round of applause because that is not as easy as it looks. Congratulations! With talent like that, you actually have many, many skills to offer the world.

I encourage you to take this opportunity to look at this as a fresh start. It's a brand new, clean slate. You can do whatever you want! I'm living proof! I completely started my life over once my twins graduated high school.

This was an opportunity for me to look at my life as it was. I was a single women 'empty nester', living in a five-bedroom house. Is that really where I wanted to be? I had planned to move back to California at some point after the divorce since my family lives there. I moved to Chicago all those years ago for love and marriage, but that wasn't my life anymore. I lived away from my family for 24 years. I wanted to get back near them, and I wanted to go back to the warmer weather. I couldn't bear (pun not intended) the Chicago weather another moment.

After looking at my options, I decided I was going to do whatever was necessary to make it happen. It took almost a year to plan, but where there's a will, there's a way. I thought carefully about it. I just knew I couldn't be living in Chicago while my kids were off to college in other states. So, I saved what I could, planned carefully, and then…I LEAPED! I mean, who does stuff like that? With two kids heading off to college, I quit my high paying corporate job of twenty years, I sold the house that I lived in for twenty years, and I sold all of my belongings! I moved cross country from Chicago to San Diego with boxes! I rented a furnished vacation rental at the beach for nine months so I could just start "living" right away. I wanted to get the lay of the land and figure out ultimately where I wanted to settle down. I loved it so much! I could see the ocean from my deck and hear it when I slept. It was heaven on earth! I have not looked back. Not once. The only part that's difficult is that my children now have parents in different states. But, we are making that work. My children are extraordinary. They are so supportive of me. And, I KNOW this was the right decision. I had to follow my heart and my dreams. If I stayed back, it would be because of them. That would teach them that their dreams don't matter and that they need to put the needs and desires of others above their own. Never! They see through me that our happiness is incumbent upon us to do for ourselves.

If someone would have said to me five years ago that I would be an inventor, an author, an entrepreneur with two companies, living in San Diego, I would have said NO WAY! Look where life took me. Incredible. And it just keeps getting better and better. I want that for you! I want every day of your life to be better than the day before—whatever that is for you!

I took the leap. I'm not encouraging you to do anything nearly as drastic. However, just know that you CAN. Make sure when you get to the end of your life, your wishes and dreams are fulfilled. If you don't like where you live, move! If you want to travel, book a trip! If you want to take salsa lessons, do it! There isn't anything you can't do or have. You are so worth it and deserving.

This time of your life is ending, but it's also a new beginning which is exciting, fun and unknown! It's mysterious, and it should be spontaneous, rich and full!

If you are saddened by the "empty nest" syndrome, you can create a new passion, find a new purpose, and put that smile on your face again and do it in a way that would probably even surprise you.

Exercise:

Here are three small tips if you are feeling like you have time on your hands and don't really know what to do with it.

First, write out a bucket list.

If you haven't already, this is a great time to do it. Just have fun with it and don't leave anything out! Make it as long and extensive as you want.

Second, I encourage you to explore meet-up groups and expand your circle of friends. There are groups for everything. Just plug in a couple of topics that you find interesting, and a whole slew of opportunities of meeting new people and joining new groups will pop up for you. Most meet up groups are free.

Third, I would encourage you to look at one thing that you might have always wanted to do in your life but never had the chance to do…usually because of timing. Then, just do it! Take the action! Say yes to you! Paint the picture, learn to fly, volunteer, learn a new language, whatever it is…just do it! No more excuses!

There you have it…three simple things you can do right now to create more passion in your life, to help you on your journey to finding purpose, and ignite a permanent smile on your face.

In this chapter we learned:
• Feeling lost after children leave the home.
• Identify what you can give to the world.
• Create opportunities to meet new people and groups.

YOUR HEALTH

This should really be near the front of the book because it's that important. We all have bodies, every single one of us, and we have to take care of ourselves.

How are you "showing up" in your life regarding your health? Are you watching what you eat, are you exercising, are you limiting your intake of substances that could be damaging to you?

We need to be doing things on a regular basis that are enhancing our bodies. We do so by creating a healthy lifestyle. I am passionate about this because our health is everything. You could have all the money in the world, but if you don't have your health, you have got nothing. Who wants to live unhealthy or in pain? Not me.

I take time for myself every single day to exercise. It might be just a walk some days, but I move my body every single day. I am also conscious about what I put in my body.

It is my personal preference but, I don't eat meat. I eat fish, eggs and vegetables mainly. I limit things like dairy and sugar. I don't say that I never have them, but I limit them to only rare special occasions.

I love wine. I really love red wine. I have a glass or two almost every night. Red wine has health benefits, so I don't feel bad indulging in it.

So, here we go with another three-step process for you.

Step One: Keep a record of what it is you are ingesting in your body. Are you making smarter choices? For example, could you have ordered the salad at McDonald's instead of the burger?

Decisions like that matter. Most women who have a few pounds to lose (their words, not mine) would benefit from writing down what they eat for a week. It's not to be a food Nazi with yourself....it's to create awareness of what you're putting in your body. I think you will find that you are consuming way more calories than you think you are. It can get away from us, and all of those little bites and treats here and there, those couple of extra calories in every single day, can add up to ten pounds in a year in nothing flat! Believe me, I know!

So, write it down—by hand or digitally. Download one of the many apps that calculates it all for you. That's so easy to do. It takes no effort at all. Then, see where the extra calories are sneaking in.

Step 2: Replace instead of remove. If you drink coffee in the morning with cream and sugar and you love your morning coffee but don't want to give it up, replace the cream and sugar with one of the many varieties of options these days! Stevia and coconut milk are delicious in my morning coffee. I use a handheld frothing device, and then I use my Spifter to top off my coffee with a perfect sprinkle of cinnamon. I get a barista experience at home every single day. Howard Schultz would be so proud. Not only that...it's delicious! I don't miss the cream or sugar at all! (If you want more information on purchasing The Spifter, please go to www.amazon.com or to our site directly.) It's small, permanent changes that create lasting results.

Step Three: Exercise. No Excuses! Put it on the calendar and make it non-negotiable. This is your life and your health! Just do it! You KNOW you feel better afterwards. Exercising is 90% getting there and 10% effort. It's so true. Find something you like because you're more likely to go and do it.

We all love the results of exercising. We feel so much better. Our clothes look and feel so much better, and we live longer. Hello…this is a no brainer. Just do it already.

I'm here with you, believe me. If there was a magic pill that would allow me to sit on my butt and each chocolate and cheese all day, I'd invest every dollar I have and I could find in that pill! It doesn't exist. It's up to us, as it should be, to nurture ourselves, to take impeccable care of our bodies that work so hard to carry us around everywhere. The least we could do is show it some respect. Just sayin'.

Don't beat yourself up if you fall backwards here and there. Just remember the next morning to wake up and say the "I HAVE TODAY" poem. Because you do have that moment to start fresh and new.

In this chapter we learned:
• Taking time for your health.
• Eating healthy, watching calories.
• Calendar your exercise.

How are your showing up with Money?

How are you showing up with money in your life? Are you happy with the amount of money you have? Are you saving some and spending some? Do you have any passive income flowing into your life? How educated are you about money?

Money is such an issue for so many of us. We have a lot of resistance around it. We have these thought patterns that are the result of old programming within us. So many of us think money is for some people and not for others. We believe that it's bad and greedy to want money! How crazy is that?

The truth is there is an unlimited amount of money available! It is LIMITLESS! SO much money, SO much abundance available for the entire world! Money is simply energy, just like everything else. The truth is that 95% of "money" is digital, electronic, on paper or a computer screen. Only 5% of money is actual paper and coins. It's our limiting beliefs about our value and our self-worth that allows money to either flow into and stay away from our lives. So, how you "show up" with money will depend on how much of it comes into your path and your life.

Let's get real here, be honest with yourself. Do you see yourself as worthy and deserving, or are you riddled with feelings of lack and scarcity? My goal is to empower you so that you KNOW how worthy and deserving you truly are.

We all need the knowledge and tools to be able to make it out on our own, no matter what our current situation is. Things happen, life changes, and we need to be prepared for anything.

There are so many ways to earn money—different silos, different avenues…working, saving, investments, passive income streams, etc. In order to figure out where you're going, you have to know where you are. Below is a simple, three-step exercise to help you figure that out.

Step One: Take a look at your current spending. Write down everything you spend money on for 30 days. Your cup of Starbucks every morning, your lunches, tickets to the movies, online purchases, everything. Add this list to the bottom of your monthly obligations, like rent, utilities, groceries, gas, car payment, etc.

Step Two: Once you have that list of additional spending items, look at that list and ask yourself these questions: "Do I pay myself first? Am I putting enough money away? How can I spend this money better?"

Step Three: Have this conversation with yourself on a regular basis. By doing so, you'll create a new habit and a better awareness of how you value yourself and your money. You'll start shifting some of the ways you spend money, and all of a sudden, the bank account will start going up. It's magical. It's easy. Just by focusing "good" energy, you will attract more and more abundance.

This is all about building momentum in your life...positive momentum. Slow, steady steps. Simple. Easy. Everything is easy as one, two, three.

Money is good! And you deserve ALL that you desire! Keep that in mind every day. You are so worth it!

In this chapter we learned:
• Money is not only for some people.
• Looking at how we spend money, can we spend it in a better way?
• The importance of paying ourselves first.

PARENT WITH PEACE

Let's cover the topic of parenting with peace. I know how challenging this can be at times. I'm the mother of twins, and if any of you are the parent of twins, or have multiple children, you know what I'm talking about. It's full of challenges.

Communication really becomes challenging as our kids enter the teen years and into young adulthood. This is when they really begin to develop their personalities and independence. This is when you get those comments and looks, and you know they're thinking 'she has no idea what she is talking about and I couldn't hate her more right now!'

It can create a really volatile environment because it's as if you're speaking two totally different languages. That's actually what is happening. In many instances, our kids literally can't even hear us. For example, did you ever notice HOW MANY times you have to ask them to take out the trash? You say it over and over again, each time getting louder and louder, until finally you're shouting and so upset about it. They look at you like you're insane and wonder why you're getting so upset about something so trivial. OK, can anyone out there relate to this? The higher and higher the volume of your voice goes, the less they can actually hear you and are able to listen to you.

I know that I've experienced a similar scenario in my household dozens, if not hundreds, of times in my life. Therefore, I discovered a way to communicate with my children that I call "Parenting with Peace." Once I figured out that we are not speaking the same language, I realized I had to become an interpreter and their audience. We are each individuals, and we can't possibly know what someone else is truly thinking. What I do know for sure is that we all want to be heard, acknowledged and appreciated.

When I discovered that they really just want to be acknowledged and heard, I changed my communication style and approach. Now, I stop for a moment and allow them to run with their words, let them just go "off "about whatever is going on with them (even if it's about me.) I just sit with them, creating space for them, giving them the opportunity to express themselves fully, and be their audience, which is what they need in that moment.

Once they've stopped talking, I take a breath and ask the question, "Are you done? Are you finished?" I want to make sure they've completed what they wanted to say. When the answer is yes, the next thing I say is "I hear you. I really do…and from what I heard, I am guessing you are probably *feeling* like (fill in the blank.)" It could be hurt, angry, rejected, or whatever the emotion is.

This creates a feeling of validation, "She really does hear what I am saying, she is acknowledging me, she respects me, and she understands me".

This has contributed to the wonderful open dialogue I share with my children. There is nothing that they can't come and talk to me about. Very few, if any, subjects are off limits with us. I respect them, and they respect me. They both know that they can come and talk to me about ANYTHING, and there will never be any judgment, and I always give them their space because they just want to be heard.

As parents, we sometimes forget that our children are people too. And we as people, we want to be heard and respected by our children as well…but it is our responsibility as parents to show them the way first, to create that space for them. In return, they learn by our example, and then they learn how to peacefully communicate as well.

Step One: Sit in the space and give them the room to go off about whatever is bothering them.

Step Two: Ask them if they are finished.

Step Three: Acknowledge that you heard them and tell them that you're guessing they are *feeling* like_____.

Try this exercise. Let me know how this is working for you. I'd love to hear your stories!

In this chapter we learned:
• What is parenting with peace?
• How to give space to your children for dialogue.
• We all want to be heard, acknowledged and appreciated.

DECIDE YOUR BOUNDARIES

Respecting our own boundaries is a skill worth learning on your path to your passion, purpose and smiles. It's easy for us to get caught up in the wants and desires of others. People may be coming at you all day, every day, with THEIR problems and needs. Your kids, your spouse/partner, your boss, your needy girlfriends, your mother...on and on. All of a sudden, you feel like things are piling up on you, and it becomes more difficult not to "take it in." It's draining you! It needs to stop. You do not need to be carrying around anyone else's baggage.

An effective tool for not allowing this to happen is to create healthy boundaries for yourself. So, how do you do that? Well, it's simple. There are graceful, gentle ways to say what you need to say in a respectful, tactful way. For example, let's say you're in an argument with your mom. She keeps coming at you with this and that, and you simply can't hear it anymore, and don't want to "take" this from her for another moment. But, she doesn't want to let it go.

A great way to create safe boundaries is to create some space...for you! Here's how: you might say to her, "I hear you Mom; I appreciate where you are coming from, but I can't take this on right now. And, while I appreciate and respect what you are going through and where you are coming from, I hope you will do the same for me and appreciate where I am coming from right now. I just need some space and some time. Maybe we can talk about this later or at another time under different circumstances. I am happy to do that, but right now, I have to respect my own feelings."

Another way of respecting your boundaries is the power of the word "no." If you don't want to do something, for heaven's sake, do not do it! Be less willing to say yes right away. Allow yourself the proper amount of time to process a request before responding.

Something in the moment may sound really good. But, upon further reflection, it's maybe not such a good idea. So, learn to say "no" in a respectful way. It's similar to the statement above, "I appreciate your offer, request, etc., but I'd like a little time to think about it and get back to you. I hope that you can appreciate where I'm coming from." Simple, easy, understandable. You are taking in to consideration what works and does not work for you. That's how you decide what your boundaries are.

Practice this wherever possible by asking yourself this question in any given situation. Do I really want to be doing this? Will this bring me happiness? Am I doing this out of some sense of obligation? By asking yourself questions like this, you'll start to recognize patterns of where you don't honor your boundaries, and the "lines" will become clearer.

In this chapter we learned:
• How to create safe boundaries for yourself.
• Identify what your boundaries are.
• How communication techniques create safe boundaries.

BEING SELFISH IN A REALLY GOOD WAY

I love being selfish, I really do. That may sound terrible, but not the way I mean it. When you are selfish in a really good way, you are able to serve the world with much more enthusiasm. Now, that's how to live with passion, purpose and to keep on smiling!

This is a stretch for many of us, especially women because we have become so accustomed to serving the needs of others first while putting our needs on the back burner and at the bottom of the list. That's the quickest path to feeling depleted, tired, unfulfilled and unhappy. Your needs must come first! There needs to be zero guilt about them, and you need to learn to drown out the sounds of others' criticisms, guilt trips or disapproval.

Before I list the three simple steps to this exercise, I want you to know this first. When you are selfishly loving yourself, caring for yourself, nurturing yourself, you will be emanating radiance, happiness, and joy. You will feel better about doing everything in your life. I get up every day and express my gratitude. Then, I go and do my routine of nurturing my spirit, mind and body. After that, I feel amazing and ready to take on the day! That's because I put myself first! That's the definition of being selfish in a really good way.

Step One: Take out a piece of paper and write down all the things you'd love to do on a daily basis. (Take a bubble bath, exercise, walk five miles, have "quality" morning time, etc.)

Step Two: Pick a window of time on the calendar each day that is going to work for you. (Mine is 5-7am. I get up early to do it, but I LOVE it! So, it's not hard to do.)

Step Three: Force yourself to stay committed to doing it. After only a few days, you'll feel so good about it. We know it takes 21 days to form a habit. Commit to those days and allow the routine to develop. And bask in your sacred time!

One final note…you will start to see that you have more time in your days when you make time for you. You'll just have a greater capacity for handling everything else.

So, get to it! Put YOU first. Be Selfish and Love It!

In this chapter we learned:
• How to be selfish the right way.
• How to get rid of the feeling of guilt.
• Steps to the path of being selfish in a good way.

For more information, go to www.dianeforster.com or www.ihavetoday.com. Enter your name and email address to become part of the "I Have Today" Community, and receive FREE gifts, like the "I Love You" Chant and the "I Forgive You" Chant.

FINDING YOUR PASSION

I am at what I would consider with any luck, the halfway point of my life. It took most of my life to figure out what my passion and purpose is. I knew from a very young age that being a mother was definitely one of my purposes. The most important one, actually. I am so blessed to be a mom. If nothing else ever happened to me in this life, I would be all good with God and He with me. However, something did happen. A series of events that led me to my calling. I am supposed to tell my story because it will help other women. I am writing, coaching, speaking, and letting women know that they have so much POWER within them! Not muscle power, but energy power, creative power, influential power. The reason I know this is because I discovered just how powerful I was. So, if I am this powerful, so are all of you! I learned that I can be, do and have ANYTHING! I am limited by NOTHING! NO ONE is more deserving than me, and I can't make a mistake. There are no mistakes, only lessons along the way. I can't tell you how many "lessons" I've learned along with way inventing The Spifter. Many, many, many! Yet, despite fear, doubt, worry, and a few hard knocks, The Spifter is alive and well! It's unique, it's so special to me, it has won awards, and I wouldn't trade a single experience, good or bad, from it. Because my journey with it has brought me to where I am today. A passion for cooking turned into a business in the house wares industry. Never in a million years would I have predicted that! And...my path to learn more, network more, experience more led me down the path to writing this book (my first of many I feel.) I've always loved writing. I just had so much overwhelming fear based around it. Yet, here it is!

My path to spiritual awakening, personal development, living a truly inspired life led me down the path to teach, coach and speak. Again, I didn't see any of this coming if you spoke to 25-year-old Diane. She was so different.

I share all of this with you because I know there are so many of you out there feeling a higher calling. You're feeling a pull to do more, to be more, to live more, to love your life more, to give more. I get it, I really do. I'm here to support you. I want to help you get there. I hope my story and my processes have helped you some. I hope you're doing some deep digging for yourself. I hope you'll spend some time, a lot of time, daydreaming, imaging a life so much bigger than you thought possible. It's totally possible. Look at me. I feel younger and stronger every single day. I feel more energy and more alive now than I did back in my twenties.

I am here for you. I am happy to share this story with you—my hurdles as well as my triumphs. We all have things we must overcome. To learn and grow from difficult experiences allows us to stretch and appreciate the good times even more. Don't let the dark days, and the negativity, and the stuff that brings us down define who you are. Stretch above it. Learn from it. Grow from it. Use it to enlighten someone else. Love It! Thank It! Bring It!

Thank you for allowing me to share a piece of myself with you. I'm at this point because of support like yours. It means so much. I want to hear from you! I want to know you! I want you to share your stories with me. I want the "I HAVE TODAY" community to spread globally. I want our love to be felt across the universe. I want us all to live each day to the fullest. I want us all to stay present, in the moment, to live by the motto "I HAVE TODAY!" What a gift this day is!!!

With the second half of my life left to live, I feel like I'm just getting started! On that note, you'll be hearing from me again soon. Until then, I have today. Thank you, God, for today.

In this chapter we learned:
• Diane had no idea where the road would lead.
• The dark moments that brings us down are not who we are.
• Empower others by our example.

For more information, go to www.dianeforster.com or www.ihavetoday.com. Enter your name and email address to become part of the "I Have Today" Community, and receive FREE gifts, like the "I Love You" Chant and the "I Forgive You" Chant.

WANT MORE?

'I HAVE TODAY' SYSTEM

Have you felt like you have lost your passion, your purpose? When was the last time you smiled on a regular basis? Are you tired of living a ho-hum kind of life? Do you want to ignite more passion and purpose in your life? Well, I want that for you too.

I am Diane Forster, Founder of 'I Have Today'. I have developed an amazing three-step process that is so easy to follow. It is going to transform your life, empower you, and ignite or reignite your purpose and your passion and your smile again. I call it the 'I Have Today' System.

It is a three-step process that takes you from where you are to where you want to be in ninety days, or less, guaranteed.

I went from being suicidal on my bathroom floor to breaking free from a marriage that was really difficult, empowering myself and getting to a place where I was on QVC with my own product that I invented!

Now I am on a mission to empower women with this movement to live a life that is rich, full, and passionate. Living a life with purpose will bring back and reignite the smile on their face with my simple and easy three-step process.

I have taken years to study and perfect this. Now I offer it to you. I promise you, you can change your life in as little as ninety days, or less, guaranteed. All you have to do is sign up for the program…say yes to you!

How much is it costing you NOT to participate in this? Do you want to wake up ninety days from now and be exactly where you are now? No!

Take this opportunity to do this. I have made it easy and simple for you, and you are not going to be alone. You are going to have community; you are going to have support. We are here for you; we have got your back. That's always the scary part—no one wants to do it alone. We're not meant to. We are meant to lift each other up. We are meant to hold each other accountable. We are meant to support each other.

I want you to live your life with passion and purpose and to smile as much as you possibly can. I want you wake up excited about today and looking forward to it instead of dreading it. The name of this company is "I Have Today." We are all about today. We have today and that is all we have guaranteed. Yesterday is done; it is in the past, and there is no guarantee of tomorrow.

So, I have today. Are you with me, do you want to join me?

The online program is an investment in you for an enlightened, impassioned, empowered life full of passion, purpose, and smiles— smiles from ear to ear. Let's do this. Imagine what it would feel like to wake up every day feeling alive and excited about today. Imagine what it is going to feel like when people are coming up to you and asking "What is going on with you? You look amazing, you look different, and you look so happy!"

Imagine when your partner starts looking at you and engaging with you in a whole new way. He is alive by your lightness. Imagine what it is going to be like when the relationships that you have with your children are more peaceful and cohesive.

Imagine what it is going to feel like when your relationship with money is now a positive relationship. Imagine what it is going to feel like when you get to the end of ninety days and you look in the mirror and you don't even recognize that woman. You don't even know who she is because she is such a different person than she was ninety days before. Doesn't that sound amazing and exciting?

And the process is so easy. The steps are so simple, it won't even feel like effort. I have taken into consideration your time and respect that. This will be incorporated into your life so that it will just become part of your natural routine through easy to follow rituals.

It will be fun, it will be effortless, and it will be easy. I can't wait to see you in ninety days with that smile back on your face. The smile that you can't remove, the smile that feels so good!

Don't you want your passion back? Don't you want to be excited by life, having fun, enjoying it? Don't you want to know your purpose?

You know why you are here. You know what to do. You know who you are. Don't think, just ACT! Now! TODAY! I can't wait to take this journey with you, I can't wait to see you on the inside of the 'I Have Today' System.

Chapter Summary
In this chapter we learned:
• Three-step process of "I have today" system.
• The process is easy and effortless.
• How to have more peaceful and cohesive relationships.

For more information, go to www.dianeforster.com or www.ihavetoday.com. Enter your name and email address to become part of the "I Have Today" Community, and receive FREE gifts, like the "I Love You" Chant and the "I Forgive You" Chant.

"I am committed to seeing that one billion women across the world who suffer from lack of self-worth instead experience their true divinity, power and purpose. It starts with one person at a time. Through the power of influence and example, shifts happen."

Diane Forster

38548587R00086

Made in the USA
San Bernardino, CA
08 September 2016